PRAISE FOR

MANY LOVE

♡ ～ ♡ ～ ♡

"Johnson has created an unjaded portrait of 'unconventional' love, and reading it feels like you've both been introduced to a new, exceedingly cool best friend and granted access to a kind of interpersonal, anthropological wisdom that will cause you to reevaluate every preconceived ideal you had about family and commitment. To call *Many Love* compulsively readable is a gross understatement. This book will split you wide open."

—Kristen Radtke, author of *Imagine Wanting Only This*

"Sophie Lucido Johnson is funny, feminist, smart, and, annoyingly, a very talented illustrator to boot. *Many Love* is a compassionate and convincing love story, and a must-read for anyone who feels left out by our culture's one-size-fits-all heterosexual monogamous norms."

—Katie Heaney, author of *Never Have I Ever* and *Would You Rather?*

"*Many Love* may be about polyamory, but it's just like any touching coming-of-age story—just with a bit of a different interpersonal structure. Warm, revealing, and honest, it's a welcoming read, no matter what structure for love you have in your life."

—Jen A. Miller, author of *Running: A Love Story*

"*Many Love* is funny, poignant, and valuable for any person interested in relationships—be it with lovers, friends, or oneself. With a beautiful intertwining of words and pictures, of thoughts and ideas, Sophie Lucido Johnson has crafted a personal story that's universally applicable. I have many loves for *Many Love*."

—Myq Kaplan

MANY LOVE

♡ ～ ♡ ～ ♡

A Memoir of Polyamory and Finding Love(s)

Sophie Lucido Johnson

TOUCHSTONE

New York   London   Toronto   Sydney   New Delhi

Touchstone
An Imprint of Simon & Schuster, Inc.
1230 Avenue of the Americas
New York, NY 10020

First Touchstone trade paperback edition June 2018

TOUCHSTONE and colophon are registered trademarks of Simon & Schuster, Inc.

Names and identifying details of some of the people portrayed in this book have been changed.

For information about special discounts for bulk purchases,
please contact Simon & Schuster Special Sales at 1-866-506-1949
or business@simonandschuster.com.

The Simon & Schuster Speakers Bureau can bring authors to your live event.
For more information or to book an event, contact the Simon & Schuster Speakers Bureau
at 1-866-248-3049 or visit our website at www.simonspeakers.com.

Manufactured in the United States of America

1   3   5   7   9   10   8   6   4   2

Library of Congress Cataloging-in-Publication Data

Names: Johnson, Sophie Lucido, author.
Title: Many love : a memoir of polyamory and finding love(s) / Sophie Lucido Johnson.
Description: New York : Touchstone, 2018.
Identifiers: LCCN 2017059117 | ISBN 9781501189784 (paperback)
Subjects: LCSH: Johnson, Sophie Lucido. | Non-monogamous relationships. |
Love. | Sex customs. | BISAC: BIOGRAPHY & AUTOBIOGRAPHY / Personal
Memoirs. | FAMILY & RELATIONSHIPS / Love & Romance. | SOCIAL SCIENCE /
Sociology / Marriage & Family.
Classification: LCC HQ980 .J66 2018 | DDC 306.84/23--dc23 LC record available
at https://lccn.loc.gov/2017059117

ISBN 978-1-5011-8978-4
ISBN 978-1-5011-8979-1 (ebook)

for hannah & derek

8 toulouse street

Contents

PART 4

Let's Talk About Sex

101

PART 5

Many Love

117

PART 8
Bird-Watching

211

Choose Your Own Romantic Adventure

My boyfriend and I were on our third date with another couple when our cat Jean died.

That's not quite accurate: we were chopping up cucumbers and avocadoes for a romantic DIY sushi night with Tony and Meg when our cat's legs collapsed beneath him. I met Meg through work—a place where you are traditionally quiet about being in the kind of relationship in which you and your partner could be dating another couple. But after I left my job, Meg and I stayed friends on Facebook, and Facebook is a considerably less private sphere. On social media, I'm out as being polyamorous—that is to say, I practice ethical, consensual nonmonogamy. Meg messaged me one night to tell me that she was poly, too. "Let's be friends, possibly?" she wrote. "Or feel free to ignore this message; I promise not to find it rude if you choose to."

Meg had been my superior at work, and from the moment I met her I had a big, fat, unprofessional crush on her. She wrote scathing, intelligent news analyses (superhot when you're a writer), and she had a dexterity to her walk; later I would find out she was into circus arts and acroyoga. So, months later, after I'd left the job and figured I would probably never see Meg again, I was dizzy to get a message from her. I responded that, uh, yes, we should totally be friends, I mean, ha ha, I'm not *weirdly eager* or anything; I'm, like, superbusy, but if she wanted to, you know, I would like to . . . whatever. Somehow, through the grace of the universe, this rambling spurt of a reply didn't drive Meg away, and a few weeks later, she came over for dinner.

At dinner, I tried to act cool and look Meg in the eye a few times, but it was difficult, because she was even more beautiful and interesting than I had remembered her being. Luckily, my boyfriend, Luke, was also there, and he quelled the tension. He's a pro at asking good questions ("What's the weirdest thing you've ever done for love?")— it's one of the things I loved the most about him when we met. Regardless of the presence of a third person, though, I still felt like I was on a date with Meg. Luke knew I had a crush on her; if *she* didn't know I had a crush on her, then she was (mercifully) ignoring a few pretty obvious signs. I think the vibe was felt around the table.

We went to the sex party, which was amazing. I'm sure you have a lot of questions about the sex party (such as, "What *is* a sex party, exactly?"), and I promise that, eventually, I will answer them. But this part of the book is about my cat, who left the world before his time, and the people who were there to care for us in his wake.

At the sex party, we met Tony, who is one of Meg's partners (the one she lives with). We also, technically, met Meg's other partner and a host of people Meg dates or has dated or plays with from time to time. But Luke and I both felt drawn to Tony, who was refreshingly forthcoming. A week later, Meg asked if Luke and I wanted to go on a date with her and Tony, and we both thought that sounded great.

If I had been nervous about my friendly initial dinner with dreamy Meg, I was a *wreck* about going on an actual date with her and her partner. It was especially terrifying to embark on dating another couple *as* a couple—territory neither Luke nor I had any practice with or guidelines for. At the end of the date, if I wanted to kiss Meg or Tony or both of them, did I ask? Did we all have to kiss the first kiss together, in a kind of Spring Break–style quadrilateral?

The date was really like any other date: We ate dinner and learned about one another. We asked questions about childhood; we told stories about past loves. There was kissing at the end, and while I'd love to get into that right now in detail, I'm telling you about this date right here and now only because I want you to know, at least marginally, the nature of our relationship with Meg and Tony before I tell you about the night Jean passed away.

Everything was nearly ready for our date that night: the sushi rice had been cooked and was cooling, and the seaweed was artfully arranged on a red plate. I'd even tempered some chocolate and was dipping butter cookies in it for dessert. When Jean's legs collapsed, I called the vet, hoping he would say something like, "Oh, yeah, cats' legs collapse all the time. That's normal. Give him three sips of water and he should be good as new." But instead, he said that we needed to take him to the emergency room immediately. So Luke got the cat carrier, and I called Meg.

I should pause to say that while people who have cats are generally a little crazy about them, I am *high* on the spectrum of this feline-related lunacy. I buy food for my cats that costs significantly more than the food I buy for myself. When I go out of town, I call the cat sitter and ask to speak to my cats on the phone. Jean was one of a pair; Puppy, the other cat, seemed deeply troubled by Jean's sudden collapse, and that felt like another major crisis that had to be dealt with.

"Come over," I told Meg distantly. "Call Tony and tell him what happened, and when you get here, we'll sort it out."

I told Luke to take Jean to the vet and to call me when he got there, and we would go from there.

When she came into the apartment, Meg didn't even take off her coat before she held me tightly in her arms. "What do you need," she said, making it a statement, not a question; like she was going to do whatever it took to make this situation better and easier. I didn't have words. I just let her hold my hands.

Tony arrived just as Luke called from the vet. I shut myself in the bedroom and took in the bad news: it was a heart condition, and it was serious, and they didn't know if Jean would make it.

When I left the bedroom to tell Meg and Tony, I couldn't get the words out.

The second time I said it, Meg seemed to grasp the subtext: I *needed* them to stay. I needed someone to be with Puppy; I needed someone to hold us to the ground.

Tony and Meg made the sushi. When we had to pay an ungodly amount of money for the procedures Jean required, I called Meg and had her find my emergency credit card and read the number to me over the phone. When we got home, exhausted, defeated, and in total despair, they were still there. They stayed. They cleaned. When they finally left, holding us both a little longer than normal during their good-byes, I thought to myself, "This is what love is."

FAQ

My friends ask me a lot of questions about polyamory. Some of them are ridiculous—"Since you're poly, won't you condone my cheating on my husband?"—and some are not. Chances are, if you're reading this book, you have a few questions, too. To help get things off the ground, let's get a few of them out of the way.

What is polyamory? Isn't it just a failure to commit?

There's a whole camp of people—many of whom are my relatives, fearfully praying for my soul when I say I'm polyamorous—who think that polyamory is about having sex with whomever you want, whenever you want, without a whole lot of emotional consideration. This definition is all wrong. "Poly" comes from the Greek word for "many," and "amory" comes from the Latin word for "love"; literally, the word means "many love." When I say that I'm polyamorous, that is what I mean: I have many loves. I am *deeply* committed to my loves. When I have sex, I do it with emotional consideration and communication, because loving someone means being com- passionate about the way they feel, and that can be complicated when jealousy is involved. But to me, polyamory is not really about sex at all. It's not "many sex," it's "many love." The love I hold for my closest friends, with whom I do not sleep, is an enormous part of it. Polyamory is about shifting my definition of love to embrace the diversity of relationships in my life, and about allowing myself to prioritize *all* of those relationships according to their demands.

Late for what? * Rory?

* I'm going to call ALL
the fictional characters
in this book, Rory,
because I LOVE "The
Gilmore Girls."

I'm embarrassed about
this, but this book is
about honesty.
        I want to be honest
            with you.
    We all LOVE
things we are
    ashamed of.

Love is infinite. This shouldn't even be controversial. There is nothing more beautiful about the human species than our capacity to love; as a society, we've come a long way in the versions of love we accept. But saying "Yeah, our girlfriend Meg and our boyfriend Tony are going to come to the beach with us this weekend" raises eyebrows nevertheless. It can still be hard to have conversations about polyamory because there is something very fixed in the modern mind-set about how relationships ought to look— i.e., monogamous. Conversations with my friends about polyamory often go like this:

Are you out? What does your family think?
I mean, aren't you ashamed?

I don't have much of a choice in the matter, because I decided to write a book about it. Everyone in my family had the annoying habit of wanting to know what the book was about. For a while, I just said, "It's a book about love." This led people to believe that I was entering the seemingly limitless field of women's romance novels. As much as I do someday hope to write a book titled *The Man Stallion of the Dude Ranch of Shangri-La*, I felt I was misleading people. I slowly started to tell those I trusted most in the world that the book was actually about polyamory—a statement that was almost always met with a deflated "Uh-huh" and a quick change of subject.

I get it. I used to feel exactly the same way. A few years ago, my friend Leslie was dating an attractive guy who openly had another girlfriend, and I thought it was fucked up. I told Leslie all the time that she deserved better than that; it was hard to see a guy dating (and sleeping with) two different women—and doing so without trying to hide any of it—as anything other than misogyny. And maybe that guy *was* being misogynistic, I don't know; I wasn't in that relationship. Looking back, the fact that Leslie had to compromise what *she* really wanted (to be monogamous) in order to be with that guy sends up a few red flags for me.

But a few years later, when my roommates (who were dating) started to talk about being in a polyamorous relationship, it seemed different, because they were so open and conversational about it; communication and transparency were at the center of the whole dynamic. As I listened to their conversations on the topic (read: as I pretended to look at magazines in the living room with headphones on while they chatted candidly in the adjacent room), I started to think that maybe there were aspects of this relationship style that would work for me, too. Until that point, I'd believed polyamory was all about sex; now, I started to see it as a pretty versatile relationship structure.

Just a note, though, specifically for my Grandma Bev: There's a whole chapter in here that's about sex. It's clearly labeled. In that chapter, I do talk candidly and at some length about sex. You, Grandma Bev, should skip that chapter. I love you.

What's your favorite book about polyamory?

No question about it: Deborah Anapol's *Polyamory in the 21st Century.* I will cite it roughly one million times over the course of the next few hundred pages. Poly blogger Alan M. (a lot of self-identifying polyamorous people don't reveal their last names because they hold corporate jobs, and, unfortunately, it's not always socially acceptable to be polyamorous) notes that it "was often called [polyamory's] bible."[1]

Guys, this book is *great.* Here is just one teensy tiny sample: "Polyamory has more to do with an internal attitude of letting love evolve without expectations and demands than it does with the number of partners involved."[2] *Right?* Isn't that *beautiful*?

A Little More on Deborah Anapol and Her Cohort

Anapol, who died unexpectedly in 2015, had a PhD in clinical psychology, and she used what she knew about the human brain to make living in this world a little kinder, easier, and better all around.

I mention the PhD because Anapol and her cohort can come off as sort of New Agey: she was a major player in an organization called Loving More, which still holds retreats and talks about "pelvic heart floors" and the like. The person who allegedly popularized the term "polyamory" in the 1990s called herself (and I am not making this up) Morning Glory Zell-Ravenheart. I know how all of this sounds, and I, too, tend to shrink away from any movement that might employ words like "vibrations" or "aura" in day-to-day practice.

I talked to Alan M. on the phone recently; he's been an on-again, off-again polyamorist for almost fifty years. Alan, who is sixty-four, is gentle and soft-spoken; he also seems to know everything there is to know about polyamory—and he knows how New Agey some of the people in the movement can seem. Speaking specifically about an annual summer retreat in the woods, Alan told me, "This sounds like New Agey hoo-ha, but of all the New Agey–type things I've seen, this has more intellectual integrity than what's generally out there." In fact, a lot of people who are at the forefront of polyamorist efforts have hard-science backgrounds. Alan described them as "experimenters."

I liked talking to Alan. He and many of his compatriots in the Loving More community, who have been studying and practicing this kind of relationship model for decades, are a little skeptical about the so-called next generation of polyamorists. In a speech Alan gave at the 2016 Rocky Mountain Poly Living Conference in Denver, he said, "I keep hearing disturbing ways that the word 'polyamory,' as it spreads, is being used out there as just a hip-sounding new term for old-style screwing around without regard for other people." This must be particularly frustrating, as Alan and people like him have been practicing some version of nonmonogamy for decades—and they're still doing it.

Actually, the folks at Loving More do a bunch of events. THE BIG ONE IS The Annual Poly Living Conference, which is your basic come-one-come-all hotel conference. Age groups (between 21 & the late 70s) are actually ALL pretty well represented, according to Loving More's data. Everyone — poly, not poly, single, paired, throupled, whatever — is WELCOME. no pun intended, I promise

The Loving More Retreat, on the other hand, is an "experience in polyamory, community." Everyone lives together and eats together, & clothing is optional.

I know you said polyamory isn't only about sex, but **isn't it?**

Hey, don't take *my* word for it. Even sex columnist Dan Savage, who gets a lot of credit for popularizing the practice of polyamory for a new generation (Savage and his husband are famously "monogamish"), says that polyamory isn't about just sex for him.

"Because we were a gay couple when we came out as being in an open relationship, people made a lot of assumptions about our sex life," Savage told me. "Everyone seemed to think we were kind of slutty—and not always in a bad way, because we run in a very sex-positive crowd. People thought we were just going out all the time and picking up as many random guys as we could; they thought we were inviting strangers into our house constantly. But that's not how it was at all; we were sleeping with each other more than with anyone else. We were more monogamous than not. So it became clear that being in an open relationship was a spectrum." He added that most of the men he and his husband sleep with are regulars; they're people Savage and his husband consider part of the family, so to speak.

How is polyamory different from open relationships?

We will talk *a lot* about this, so don't worry. But here's my short answer: if relationship models were geometrical shapes (bear with me), open relationships would be rectangles, and polyamorous relationships would be squares. By that I mean all polyamorous relationships are open, but not all open relationships are polyamorous. An open relationship is simply a nonmonogamous one; a polyamorous relationship requires a specific kind of commitment to the people with whom one is romantically involved. Polyamory requires transparency, communication, and enthusiastic consent. Open relationships embrace polyamory, but they might also include relationships centered on dating around, or don't-ask-don't-tell relationships.

In my own experience, people are very quick to make the leap from "open" to "slutty" without a whole lot of examination. Savage has a newspaper column and a podcast that are mostly about sex; as he has come to be a sort of poster child for the modern-day polyamory movement, I can understand why people might equate polyamory with sex. I'm of the opinion that there is nothing wrong with wanting to jump into bed with tons of people—so long as everyone is communicative and responsible and everything is consensual. That isn't, however, how all polyamorous people—or even *most* polyamorous people—live their lives. Savage told me that he feels sad for people who think the poly lifestyle is "about fucking and nothing else." For Savage and his husband, polyamory is about building meaningful and lasting relationships with people inside and outside of their primary partnership.

So you're saying everyone should just throw their wedding rings in a nearby creek and be polyamorous; is that it?

No, I don't think polyamory is for everyone. I don't believe that if couples were to open up their relationships and love freely, the world would automatically be a better place. People are different, and as such, they love differently. The characters of Cory and Topanga from the TV show *Boy Meets World* are not cut out for a polyamorous relationship, and the (fictional) world is better for it. (More on that later.) But I do think polyamory is right for me.

Is this book a memoir? Is it a research-y type of book? Is it a pop-up book? Where are the pop-ups?

This book is, mostly, a personal exploration of polyamory. It's about my own small journey through the good, the bad, and the

ugly relationships that led me to live with a partner, regularly visit another long-distance partner, and redefine for myself what the word "partner" really means. I've also included some anthropological and anecdotal research that I found helpful while choosing my own romantic adventure.

Aren't you a thirtysomething bisexual white woman whose experiences are mostly heterosexual? Isn't that a narrative we've all already heard?

Totally, and thank you for bringing it up! I've enjoyed a lot of privilege in my experiences around choice.

When I asked the people in my life who know a lot about polyamory to suggest words that would be good to clearly define in a book like this, a lot of their answers had to do with privilege. Here are just a few of the many terms that are important to know and pay attention to when talking about polyamory:

Class privilege: With the choice to be polyamorous comes the need to be flexible with one's time. That isn't always possible, particularly for people who aren't paid a living wage. Having multiple partners is a privilege that, like so many things in our world, is not afforded to everyone.

Heteropatriarchy: This is a term coined to describe a social system that favors men and heterosexuality over women, gender-nonconformists, and people with nonstraight sexual orientations. The heteropatriarchy is why so many of the polyamorous relationships that are visible in the media are ones in which a man in a relationship with a woman asks to open it up, and the woman agrees. In my conversations with women over the course of writing this book, I found that the vast majority were frustrated with the way polyamory has been conveyed in the media. Stories about functional nonmonogamy are rarely about the desires of women, and it's even rarer for those stories to feature women primarily dating other women.

Transphobia: Many people worldwide express profound dislike for transgender and transsexual bodies. This dislike and fear leads to a skewed representation of the sorts of people who are "allowed" to be in polyamorous relationships.

White privilege: On television shows about polyamory like *You, Me, Her* and *Polyamory: Married & Dating*, one thing is automatically and abundantly clear when it comes to casting: poly folks are pretty much universally depicted as white. Because of racial privilege, it's possible for white people to enjoy alternative relationship models without facing the same kind of persecution marginalized racial populations do. Whiteness makes it easier to go public with alternative relationship structures because white people face less judgment and oppression overall. Most of the people I'm dating are white. While there are a few people of color at the poly cocktail events in my very diverse city of Chicago, the folks who come out are overwhelmingly white. It's crucial to note that being "out" as poly is more dangerous for some people than it is for others, and, sadly, the level of danger often runs along racial lines.

One of my intentions in writing an account like this is to flex the possibilities of what can be meant by the word "relationship"—in other words, how can our friends be a part of our love lives? Women loving other women are at the center of this exploration for me, but be warned that most of the sex discussed here is, nevertheless, predictably heterosexual. To that end, I should also mention that in working on this book, I found again and again that much of the scientific research on love, sex, sexuality, and polyamory involves mainly socially dominant population groups. I wish this weren't true, but it is. I apologize on behalf of my species.

＊these are all the people I've called "boyfriend" or "partner." There are many, many more I have loved.

(THESE ALL LASTED BASICALLY 1.5 YEARS. ONLY A FEW OUTLIERS.)

Eli 2002-2003

BEN 2003-2004

MAC 2004-2006

RORY 2006-2007

SEAN 2007-2008

Rory II 2009

SAM 2009-2011

Jesse, 2012

Sean, season 2 2013-2014

Jaedon 2014-2015

Luke 2014-present

BOB 2015-present

Have you ever even been in a long-term, monogamous relationship?

Hey, I've dated *a lot*. And when I say "dated," I mean it in the least casual way possible: I've had a ton of boyfriends, and I stayed with them all for long periods of time—long enough to consider marriage. Because I don't want to waste your time, I'm writing about only a few of these relationships—specifically, I'm writing about the ones that helped me, if inadvertently, stumble into the whole polyamory thing. On the previous page, I've provided a comprehensive time line of the people I've seriously dated in my life. This is important because, time-wise, I jump back and forth a bit in this book. Feel free to refer back to the time line if you ever feel confused. The drawings are extremely accurate, so if you see these people on the street, try not to be too obvious about knowing who they are.

PART 1

Happily Ever After?

I learned about love from my parents. They have the model nuclear relationship: they're still married (forty-eight years and counting), they have two children, they've pretty much always had a dog and a cat (or two cats, depending on my mom's zeal for cats at any given time), and they own the house they live in on a quiet street in a pleasant neighborhood in Portland, Oregon. I don't think either of them believed they would end up nested inside the house-husband-wife-kids model; they were both sort of rebels when they were younger, attending UC Berkeley in the late 1960s and doing all the things that came with that (pot, parties, and protests). But getting married, it seems, changed things for them.

My parents got married when they were twenty. They'd been dating off and on, but my mom wanted to travel internationally, and she felt that if she was going to travel with a man, it would be prudent to tie the knot. She was a progressive woman, but she still didn't feel that women and men should be gallivanting across the country all are-they-or-aren't-they. My dad, as the story goes, was not ready to get married. So my mom said she would go to Japan without him. He said that was fine. While she was in Japan, she got a job as a model (a model! *that* wasn't hard to live up to or anything) and met a lot of nice-looking men who were interested in her. She sent my dad pictures of herself in scandalous skirts with her legs curled around chair legs or propped up on counters, and wrote notes on the backs of them: "Hiroji took this picture of me."

My dad flew to Japan as soon as he had the money, bought a flea-

1

market wedding band, and proposed. A boat captain on a cruise ship married them on their way to Russia. Then they hitchhiked across Europe married, the way my mother believed people who traveled together ought to be.

Like I said, my mom is a progressive woman, but there were still a lot of "ought to"s that she held on to from her own upbringing. You ought to clear the table after dinner if you did not cook the dinner. You ought to send thank-you notes for everything from a birthday card to a phone call on Christmas. You ought to offer to pay when you go out for lunch with anyone, even if you can't really afford it and *they* invited *you*, because it's polite to offer. And every romantic prospect ought to be at least in the running to be "The One." There is really no point in dating if you can't see a potential long-term future with the person.

So when I told my mom that I was in love with Kent Jackson in second grade, she told me that he was definitely "marriage material." She started calling him "The Big Mr. K" and asked me what we would name our kids. All my elementary school girlfriends also discussed marriage with the same fervor that they discussed Polly Pocket and grape Capri Sun (which is to say, a lot). In fact, I lost my best friends in third grade because it came out that I (still) wanted to marry Kent Jackson, and one of my best friends *also* wanted to marry him, and our friendship could not survive this potential conflict of interest.

My mom talked about love more than most moms probably did, though. The Big Mr. K was a constant topic of conversation, and she also had a habit of talking about other mothers' marriages. Once, in the car on the way to Baskin-Robbins when I was eight, she began ranting about all the other moms her age who were getting divorces.

And then there was the subject of birds.

My mom was (and is) an avid bird-watcher, and I grew up learning the more technical names of "little brown jobs," as they are commonly called (sparrows, wrens, finches, that kind of thing). Central to the conversation about birds, for my mom, was the subject of their mating habits—especially how birds, model citizens that they were, mated for life. This was a very big deal. It was repeated in the morning as we sat around the bird feeder, and it was repeated on vacations to places like Wisconsin or California, where there were new and exotic sorts of birds. All birds mated for life, and we humans ought to take note.

I worshiped my mom. I tried to do everything she did when I was growing up. When my mom told me that I should marry Kent Jackson, for example, I got it into my head that I *had to* marry Kent Jackson, or I would be letting my entire family down. At a very young age, I clung to my mom's obsession with birds, and I loved the stories about how they mated for life. Today, I even have a bunch of bird tattoos. (I know, I know: how very *Portlandia* of me. I liked birds before they were hip, okay? I was six years old when I started to love them.) I got the first tattoo after a man I had decided to marry dumped me unceremoniously over the phone. The bird was meant to symbolize my ability to find mate-for-life-style love, regardless of this traumatic breakup.

The trouble with worshiping birds for their model relationship-having skills is that birds *don't*, generally, mate for life. Most birds, according to scientists, are socially monogamous. Another way to describe that would be to say that they are *functionally* monogamous: they form pairs and work together to raise their young, but they certainly "date around," to say the least. The father of a female bird's babies isn't necessarily the male bird who helps rear them; likewise, that socially monogamous mate might very well have eggs in someone else's nest on the other side of town. Sometimes a mother bird will even lay her eggs in someone else's nest. Once the eggs (no matter whose they are) have hatched, a male and a female bird work together for a season to feed the babies and protect them from harm. They are not, however, sexually faithful. Birds are not the species of fairy-tale love after all; they simply can't raise their families alone.

My parents are still married, which is a feat, considering that people who get married between the ages of twenty and twenty-four make up the highest percentage of divorced couples in the United States.

Their marriage has not been, by any stretch of the imagination, easy. My mom, who was at the top of her class in her PhD program, moved across the country from New York to Oregon when my dad got a job at a college in Portland. She became a banker and worked her way up into increasingly powerful and lucrative positions. She hadn't necessarily dreamed of working at a bank, but she liked the way people looked at her when she gave them a business card. When she was thirty-six—which was, especially then, a little late in the game—she thought that it was time to have a baby. My parents tried and failed for a while, then decided to get a dog instead. They loved the dog so much, though, that my mom said she wanted to redouble the baby-making efforts, and when they were thirty-eight, my parents succeeded.

My mom kept working for a while after I was born, but she had a second child two and a half years later (children ought to have siblings, she said), and things got more difficult. She was promoted at the bank, and for a time, my dad was tasked with watching the kids. But my dad never wanted to watch the kids. *He* hadn't actually wanted to have kids at all. Once, while my mom was at work, my dad accidentally let go of my baby sister's stroller at the top of a big hill, and she crashed into the guardrail at the bottom. It was a small miracle that she survived. After that, my mom felt she couldn't trust my dad to watch me and my sister anymore, and she felt cornered into quitting her job—a job, she told me years later, that she not only loved but was also insanely good at.

A year later, my dad got a job at a college in San Diego, and my mom felt forced to uproot her life and replant her family. In San Diego, she saw a therapist who told her she didn't need my dad; she could "give him permission" to leave. So, on a beach somewhere, she told him just that. But he didn't leave, and the two of them climbed deeper into a marriage filled with ever-widening chasms and arguments sparked by short tempers. I'd hear them shouting in the kitchen; one of them would slam a dish against the counter, and the other would storm out. The tension was often palpable at dinner. We became a family that played card games at the table to avoid uncomfortable conversation.

My mom told me a lot of this just recently, and I know it's not the whole story. It's not my dad's side of the story, for one thing. Two years ago, over the holiday jigsaw puzzle, I asked my dad if there had ever been any problems in his marriage. He deflected: "Your mother is the love of my life. Do you have any idea how amazing she is?" He's in his late sixties now, and his marriage is in a radically different place than it was thirty years ago: his kids have left the house, he's retired, and my mom is the primary (and often only) person he sees every day. My dad has never been a person to talk about his feelings. In fact, he's never been a person to talk about much at all. Growing up, I seriously doubted that he remembered my birthday. It just didn't seem like raising a family in a suburban-looking house was of critical importance to him. There were times when the pain of that reality would be written plainly on my mom's face; she would get tight-lipped while scrubbing the dishes, the echo of a recent argument pinging around the dining room.

I wondered, always, if there was another way to be in love.

On a recent trip home, I discovered that my mother had brought out the diaries she kept when she was in high school. She left them in the kitchen by the toaster, maybe accidentally but probably on purpose. I read them in one sitting and marveled over how smart and weird and thoughtful she had been, even when she was young.

I was also surprised to find that her diary was full of sex. She was seeing one guy pretty exclusively at the time, but she would still go out with other guys (she even kissed them!), and she had a massive crush on the older blond who worked at the swimming pool. I had thought of my mother as a person who had only ever really been with my dad. I mean, she was *twenty* when they got married; how much romantic experience could she—the valedictorian of her high school class, who went to college on full scholarship and got into one of the most prestigious doctorate programs in the country—have really had?

She had a lot. On one page in her diary she wrote, "I think [name redacted] thinks I'm naïve. I'm not naïve. The guy in Berkeley, what's-his-name, told me I was the least naïve girl he'd ever met." She was tough; she was more self-actualized at fifteen than I am at thirty-one. She dated and fell in love fearlessly. In 1963, my mom was an experimental, thoughtful polyamorist. At the time, she called it "dating."

This was all surprising to me, because until I was a card-carrying out-of-college adult, my mom had made monogamy seem like the only viable—even *ethical*—relationship option. I felt that if I didn't get married by the time I was twenty, I would be a failure.

I thought about marriage all the time. I still wanted to marry Kent Jackson at fourteen, and finally told him I liked him. When he said he didn't like me back, I was *legitimately not sure how I was going to survive*. It was the first night in my whole life that I couldn't sleep; I stayed up through the small morning hours sobbing and watching the Home Shopping Network. (I had once liked to watch the show about rings so I could fantasize about Kent Jackson proposing to me; now that he had rejected me, I watched the show to torture myself.)

This rejection was especially bad because all the girls in my group had *just* started dating boys. We had initially become friends because we were the girls who didn't date boys in middle school; those girls, the ones who did date boys in middle school, flattened their bleached hair with irons and wore shirts from the mall that tactically let slip little flashes of their lower bellies. The girls in *my* group wore clothes from discount stores that were designed to look like they came from the mall and carried tubes of dollar lipstick in the front pockets of our backpacks that we swiped across our mouths after our moms dropped us off at school. For the longest time, we were stuck with one another and PG-13 movies where the teenage boys took their shirts off. The reason I told Kent Jackson I loved him was because my friend Kara had gotten a boyfriend, and I saw that if there was ever a moment to go for it, now was that time.

Kara's boyfriend was Jared Gamble, and it was a high feminist crime for her to date him, because Jared Gamble was the boy Nellie had a crush on. Sara was the second of us to get a boyfriend; she also dated Jared Gamble. This, of course, was after Kara broke up with Jared because, she said, she felt bad for making Nellie feel bad. Those days were an emotional minefield: there were five girls in the group, and we all had terrible things to say about one another, privately, in coded notes and whispered tones at agreed-upon times in the girls' bathroom. Then Nellie got a boyfriend, and after that Kara got another boyfriend. Would I *ever* get a boyfriend? *I didn't know. Probably not.*

That was the story I told myself, at least. My mom told me not to worry and that eventually I would find someone to marry. (That's how she framed it: "someone to marry.") And eventually, finally, I did find someone I felt was worthy. His name was Eli.

I met him at an audition for a teen theater collective; he was wearing a leopard-print collared bowling shirt, and I had recently dyed my hair fuchsia. (I remember asking the casting director if I would be allowed to keep my hair that color, to which he replied, "Oh, yeah; we want you guys to look like *teens*.") We flirted (although I didn't know then that I was flirting; I knew only that I was attracted to this boy and was intentionally finding myself next to him in group exercises) and exchanged AOL Instant Messenger screen names. We chatted online every night for a week during my allocated hour of computer time, and then he invited me to see *Shrek* at the downtown movie theater. When he kissed me (on the lips!) under the Burnside Bridge, I actively wished I could stop time. My dreams were coming true.

I knew I would be a perfect girlfriend. I had seen enough formulaic evening television to understand that women should be honest and funny and like pizza; they should peddle surprise tickets to basketball games and be good at baking; they should love dogs, laugh at jokes, and bravely hold back tears as often as possible. I daydreamed about being a girlfriend and wrote about being a girlfriend and talked to my friends about how much I wanted to be a girlfriend, so when I finally became someone's girlfriend, I knew not to complain about anything that misaligned. A good girlfriend—one who stayed in her place and didn't complain—would become a good wife. A few weeks after my mom met Eli, she told me that he, just like Kent Jackson had been at age seven, was "marriage material," which was just the incentive I needed to throw everything I had into the relationship.

Some things were going to have to change, though. Before I met Eli, I spent a lot of time with my friends—especially my friend Jessica. Before Eli, she came to my house every morning at 7:00 a.m. and we made toast from the huge loaf of artisan bread my mom always kept around. When it snowed and school was canceled, we slid down the icy hill on our binders and tried on my dad's slippers and made a stop-motion video about an oversized cookie. Every day after school, Jessica came over and we watched *The Kids in the Hall* and ate the good chips from the grocery store, sometimes dipped in mustard. We went to school dances with each other; we ordered $3 breadsticks from the pizzeria; we had sleepovers every weekend and slept on the pullout sofa bed together, staying up as late as we could to try to catch *Saturday Night Live*.

I didn't know it then, but more than all the romantic comedies I watched and women's magazines I read, being friends with Jessica prepared me for the role of excellent girlfriend.

In 1994, a pair of psychologists named Phillip Shaver and Cindy Hazan proposed that romantic relationships were essentially emotional "attachments" not dissimilar to those between parents and their children.[1] In 2002, Wyndol Furman extended the theory to suggest that friendships might be related to romantic relationships as well. In his research, he found that "these links were more consistent than those between parent-child relationships and romantic relationships."[2] Simply put, this means that friendships and romantic relationships aren't all that different—and that's science.

But I didn't know that in high school. In my mind, friends were merely placeholders on the path to a boyfriend; as soon as there was a boy to canoodle with, my friends would (obviously) take the bench. Being an excellent girlfriend (which I was) required a lot of time and energy, and this was hard for Jessica to understand. I had to spend my weekend days with Eli now, and I had to call him every night at 8:00 or he might doubt my loyalty. It wasn't that I didn't want to be Jessica's friend anymore; it was just that Eli had to be the most important thing in my life, and everything else would have to come after. I hated that she couldn't understand this; in fact, despite the fact that I went out of my way to spend what little free time I had with her, she seemed *annoyed* with me.

The solution was, obviously, that Jessica should get a boyfriend. This was actually my mom's idea; she said it would be fun for us to all go on double dates together, and Jessica would feel less left out. Lucky for Jessica, there was an excellent candidate in our fourth-period English class: Ben Stevens. Ben Stevens was sort of a fixer-upper—he wore pale khakis with pleats and socks with his sandals, and he was always quoting *The Simpsons* when it wasn't really appropriate—but he had a lot of potential. His hair was cake-frosting pink, and he played the cello in the after-school orchestra, which indicated an ability to commit. Also, he was very intelligent, and his friend group sat in the stairwell during lunch listening to liberal talk shows on a chunky FM radio with a long antenna. Most important, it was very obvious to me and to everyone in fourth-period English that Ben had a massive crush on Jessica. One day, just to confirm it, I passed Ben a note that said, "Do you like Jessica?" Ben wrote back, in the most careful, darkest writing, "I think she has the most beautiful hands."

Setting Ben and Jessica up was not as easy as it should have been. While I was sure I could coerce Ben into a casual dating situation, Jessica was harder to persuade. I talked her into one date. It went poorly.

Ben tried to kiss Jessica; she accommodated with the closed-mouth kind of thing you do with your grandmother; and that was the end of their relationship.

When she broke up with him the next day over the phone, Ben's world imploded. He was shocked to the brink of depression.

I was on Team Ben. Jessica's mother had clearly not taught her the importance of being a good girlfriend or landing a marriage-material man early on. When *I* spent time with Ben, after all, we could talk for hours. He had such interesting thoughts about the world—for instance, he secretly liked Christina Aguilera, but not Britney Spears; he thought Radiohead was biblical; he lost hours meticulously polishing catalogs of his "top ten" this or that—"Top Ten Albums from the Sixties," "Top Ten Movies with a Female Lead," "Top Ten Best Shows on VH1." Ben read books. He knew historical facts without having to look them up. My own boyfriend found historical facts uninteresting, and felt personally affronted that he was forced to read

To Kill a Mockingbird at school. How could Jessica not see what a great guy Ben was?

Since I was partially responsible for causing innocent Ben's unnecessary suffering, I spared some of my own time to spend with him. It was the least I could do. We scheduled walks together on the waterfront every Wednesday after school. I lied to Eli and Jessica, saying that I had school newspaper duties on Wednesday afternoons, because it would be too painful for both of them to know the truth. I wished I had more time, but reality was bleak.

One day the weather caved in on our Wednesday plan. Sometimes the rain in Portland is faint, and you can treat it like a friend who's tagging along; sometimes, though, the rain is tyrannical. This day brought on the latter type. Ben suggested we go to his house and watch *Back to the Future*, which I had never seen—apparently a bordering-on-criminal offense. The rain assaulted his windows and clamored unrelentingly, but his parents' house had heated floors and hallways that smelled like vanilla-and-pine cleaner. Before the movie started, we engaged in the activity central to our friendship: Ben complained about how unfair and cruel Jessica had been, and I sympathetically agreed.

"I mean, she never even kissed me; not really," he said.

"Wait," I said. "So you've never been kissed?"

"Not really."

There was only one thing to do.

Ben's lips were smaller than Eli's, or maybe it was just the way he pressed so hard with them; and his nose kept scraping my cheek like the beak of a bird. At first this was exciting; then it was wrong; then I forgot it was wrong. After it was over, I made up justifications: I had to do this for Ben. Ben was my *friend*. I was just helping him get kissed;

without me, he'd never have been kissed. Now I could go back to my boyfriend and pretend nothing had ever happened, and no one would be worse off for it.

On television at this time there was a show called *Boy Meets World*, which followed a kid named Cory as he awkwardly navigated young adulthood. Doing the right thing was hard for Cory; he thought school was lame and boring, his best friend lived in a trailer park, and he sometimes got teased because of his "Brillo Pad" hair. Through each season, even as Cory matriculated from high school to college, his teacher (Mr. Feeny) stayed the same, his best friend (Shawn) stayed the same, and his girlfriend (Topanga) stayed the same. The actress who played his sister inexplicably changed in 1996, but otherwise, Cory enjoyed practically mythological constancy.

Boy Meets World was my favorite show; I never missed an episode. My favorite subplot was the saga of Cory and Topanga, the most perfect couple imaginable. There is a whole episode in season seven devoted entirely to romantic flashbacks concerning their courtship from previous seasons. Topanga (whose name was, after all, Topanga) had wild hair and quirky eccentricities. In sixth grade, while working on a class project with Cory, she danced around his kitchen like a reed in the wind and drew a waxy red heart on her face with a tube of lipstick. Years later, Cory tells Shawn that this was the moment he fell in love with Topanga: at eleven, he knew what he wanted in a woman.

Cory and Topanga break up once in season four, because Cory kisses a flirtatious girl on a ski trip. Without each other, Topanga and Cory are virtually immobilized. They mope around in separate worlds, wishing to be together again. Luckily, Topanga kisses someone else, too (a hot intellectual from her past, while visiting a Van Gogh exhibit at the local museum); and, as we all know, a kiss from another man is all that's needed to remind a woman that she is not with her soul mate. Cory and Topanga get back together, go to college together (although Topanga also gets into Yale, nothing is ultimately more important than staying with her man), never have sex, and then get married in season seven.

Look at this genuine happiness!!!

I kept this picture pinned up on my BULLETIN BOARD.

Eli called me his "Topanga," and we decided, largely because of *Boy Meets World* (and, uh, my mom), to wait until we were married to have sex. My boyfriend's willingness to model our relationship after one on a television program indicated to me that I had done everything right. There were nights I couldn't sleep because my interests (antique books and newspaper design) did not align with my boyfriend's interests (video games and the Muppets). Then I thought about how Cory (who was into baseball and water guns) and Topanga (who followed all the rules and read every book) actually had very little in common, but they still managed to make it work. When you found your soul mate, you made it work.

But here was the problem: when I kissed Ben, it was not like when Topanga kissed the boy at the museum. For her, the kiss was a hollow dish; it contained nothing. For me, the kiss was sloppy and awkward and magical. I couldn't think about anything else, and I kept spending time with Ben, who made me mix CDs full of longing acoustic ballads and brought extra pumpkin bread to school to share with me.

The most recent data[3] on the subject says that roughly one in five hetero-sexual Americans has been unfaithful in a relationship. It's more common for men than it is for women, although gender isn't the only factor. The research on the subject is so extensive that it's almost strange:

- You're more likely to cheat with an old flame if you're a woman[4]
- You're more likely to cheat when your age ends in the number nine if you're a man[5]
- You're more likely to cheat, regardless of gender, if you're sexu-ally adventurous
- You're more likely to cheat if you have sexual anxiety (or fear that you'll be unable to perform in bed)[6]

Was this "cheating"? I wasn't sure. To this day I have never *sexually* cheated on a partner, but I've done a fair amount of secret kissing. In fact, if kissing counts, I cheated on most of my boyfriends. Every time, I went back and forth between trying to justify my actions ("I had to kiss him! He was depressed and he needed my lips to touch his lips") and drowning in utter self-loathing ("What is wrong with me? I'm the worst person who's ever lived; I'm a waste of air and space"). My mom told me that you should never tell anyone if you cheat on them. Admitting that you cheated "only serves to make you feel better" and doesn't do anything for the other person at all. Keeping the secret of cheating to yourself, my mom said, is one of the sacrifices you must commonly make in a relationship. You live with your private shame and all the lonely pain that comes with it. My mom's thinking, of course, has an implication: you cheat not because something is wrong with the relationship but because something is wrong with *you*.

I never told Eli I cheated. I never told *anyone* I cheated. When I finally broke up with Eli a full month after the adulterous kiss (I did it over the phone without really offering an explanation; he started to cry, and I hung up abruptly), the humiliation of my failure haunted me. I was unable to sleep or eat or make it through school without a meltdown, because I'd ripped up the pristine plotline of my future. I was Topanga! Eli was Cory! *WHAT HAD I DONE?!* (Side note: I recently binge-watched the Disney Channel reboot of *Boy Meets World*, called *Girl Meets World*—a show about Cory and Topanga's daughter, Riley. There's a scene in the eighth episode in which Topanga says [to her five-year-old son], "I wonder how many people the idea of Cory and Topanga has ruined." I literally shouted at my laptop, "AT LEAST ONE, TOPANGA! AT LEAST ONE!")

So my first relationship was over, and now I had a new one, with Ben. I was not a good girlfriend to Ben. I resented him for forcing me to fall in love with him, and for confirming that I was capable of such epic failure. I screamed at Ben in the living room because he couldn't understand my sadness. I yelled things like, "JUST GO AND LEAVE ME THE FUCK ALONE!" Then Ben would quietly, respectfully, leave. His leaving infuriated me. I punished him by intentionally getting into fights with him, and then making him pay for dinner.

Ben was a great boyfriend, though. His parents were the most functional adults alive. They had been in the Peace Corps and took me to the Unitarian Church with them, and on college visits to see campuses in Washington State. Once we went on a family hiking trip to Mount Rainier, where they had a cabin. Ben even had his own car (a very big deal in high school): it was a white Geo Prizm with a CD player in the console. Every Friday he drove me to see a movie at the suburban Megaplex by the train tracks, and afterward we went to the twenty-four-hour pie shop and played cards. (I had this poker deck with a nude woman on every card that I thought was very exciting to take out in public.)

My mom liked Ben, too, and told me he was marriage material before she even knew we were dating. Since she approved, and since Ben had a Geo Prizm, I decided that I would have sex with Ben— on my seventeenth birthday. The sex had been predetermined over myriad phone conversations about the logistics of losing our virginity. We had been dating for four months, and we knew we were going to get married someday (that was very important, even though we were Unitarians and Unitarians don't give a damn about when you have sex, just as long as you're "safe" and "emotionally ready"). Ben bought condoms—the expensive kind, because condoms are always breaking in after-school specials and sex-education textbooks. We practiced putting a condom on a banana to make sure we knew how to do it.

For my birthday, I asked my parents to take me to Azteca—a Mexican restaurant that was a little ways down the highway. There were dozens of Mexican restaurants that were closer to our house, but when we were younger, my sister Alexis and I always chose Azteca for birthday celebrations because of the free fried ice cream and sombrero. We hadn't been there in years because the whole thing had started to feel very little-kid-ish, and we'd begun picking more grown-up restaurants, like the Indian place downtown with the silk tablecloths.

I couldn't eat because I knew I was going to have sex in a car in just a few hours. The waiters came and put the sombrero on my head and placed a bowl of fried ice cream in front of me, and then they sang "Happy Birthday" to me in Spanish. The hostess with the wine-red apron took a Polaroid picture as a souvenir. I watched the image materialize while my sister reached over to eat my ice cream with a fork. I remember thinking that I looked very young.

this childlike human is off to lose her virginity, folks!

fried ice cream woefully out of the shot

The sex was fine. We parked in the parking lot of a trailhead where we'd made out a few times before. We went secretively into the back-seat in case there were any cops hanging around looking for teens to bust and tried fruitlessly to fog up the windows for a little while. Ben did an award-winning job with the condom; really, he looked like he could've been in an instructional video for condom application. A Geo Prizm is a small car, and I kept banging my head against the roof while the sex was happening. To tell you the truth, the sex didn't really feel like anything. It felt very similar to not having sex. I had expected it to be traumatic and emotional, but all I could think about was how much I wished my head wasn't banging against the roof of the car.

The sex-ed classes I'd taken in high school taught me that sex was going to be painful and awful; it wasn't. No one had ever told me that sex could be magical or wonderful, and so I wasn't surprised that it wasn't. Girls are not taught to feel pleasure. In her wonderful book *Girls and Sex*, Peggy Orenstein summarizes interviews she did with more than seventy young women on the subject of sex: "Listening to girls' litany of disembodied early experiences, it sometimes struck me that we'd performed the psychological equivalent of a clitoridectomy on our daughters: as if we believed, somehow, that by hiding the truth from them (that sex, including oral sex and masturbation, can and should feel fabulous) they won't find out, and so will stay 'pure.'"[7] My first time was bland, and I was taught to believe that that was as good as I could have expected it to be. I didn't think twice about the fact that Ben had an orgasm and I didn't.

We drove a few miles to an anonymous trash can to get rid of the condom. There were trash cans at the trailhead where we'd parked, but we had the idea that if we threw the condom away there, it could ultimately be traced back to us. A few months later, we drove back to the trailhead, and Ben gave me a delicate gold-chained necklace with a seed-shaped diamond (yes, a real diamond). He was a great boyfriend.

I wish I could say that the ignominy of leaving Eli faded over time. It did not. In fact, it only swelled and grew more shameful by the day, and I didn't know how to contain it. To make matters worse, Jessica was not pleased with me at all. By the time I started dating Ben, she had found a boyfriend—an Israeli musician at our school. Jessica's having a boyfriend, however, did not magically repair our friendship. She'd been cold with me since I'd started dating Ben. Now that I was with him, Ben was around all the time. I couldn't understand why this would bother Jessica. Ben was a great guy! He just hadn't been her type.

We did all go to prom together—Jessica, Jessica's new boyfriend, Ben, and me. We ate dinner at a salty Greek restaurant in Chinatown; Jessica's boyfriend had been there before and knew to order this chewy white cheese that the waiters set on fire tableside before serving it to you. Prom was on a boat. Jessica said, "I wish they could have prom on a *cloud*. I mean, a boat's fine, but a *cloud* would really be something."

At one point, Jessica grabbed my elbow while "Hey-Ya" was playing and pulled me into a narrow hallway. "You have to see Shelly Mock's makeup," she told me. Shelly, my longtime nemesis, had gone to prom with her cousin, so she was probably already having a shitty night. I peeked out at the dance floor to see her under a black light, her foundation glowing a pale green. "Forget about shaking it like a Polaroid picture," Jessica whispered. "Shelly's in a full-on darkroom."

Jessica was funnier than anyone I knew—much funnier than any boy I'd ever met. As we began to spend less time together, I noticed that I didn't laugh as much. This, I supposed, was a sacrifice one made in the name of love.

Ben and I applied to all the same colleges. We both got scholarships at a small liberal arts school in Walla Walla, where the students had been ranked "happiest" for the past five years by the Princeton Review. Jessica's dad said she had to go to a state school.

The last day I spent with Jessica before leaving for college, we went out for breakfast. "It's fine if Ben comes, right?" I'd asked. We went to a sleepy all-night diner called the Golden Touch Family Restaurant. It had vinyl-covered booths the color of avocado skin and shiny checkered tables, and waitresses with big feathery curls and gemstone makeup. They served everything on big glass platters from the 1970s and always brought out way too many tiny paper cups with balls of rubbery margarine. That was also the day Jessica's boyfriend broke up with her, because he was going to school in California and didn't think it made sense to try to date long distance. Over half a grapefruit and a plate of chocolate-chip pancakes, Jessica cried. I put my hand on her shoulder and asked, "Is there anything I can do to make you feel better?"

She looked up. Her face was as sober as a stone.

And for the record, Ben did. Ben was a good boyfriend.

It took me decades to realize what Jessica had known from the beginning: I had constructed an impossible box to live inside. The box could accommodate only two people, a man and a woman, and even then, it couldn't accommodate full versions of them. I picked the things from my mom's marriage that looked good—the house, the kids, the photo albums filled with shots of trips to Europe and anniversary dinners—and discarded anything remotely off-color. I understood that this was a challenge: I would have my mom's marriage, only better and healthier. I would have my mom's life, only fuller and richer, because I would have selected exactly the right man to shove into my tiny box life. There was no space for female friendship (who needed female friends? My mom didn't seem to have any), and there was no space for ambition outside the box (job schmob, dreams schmeams; a good husband would trump all of those). By the time I realized how unattainable this was—five boyfriends later—the damage to my female friendships had scarred over, and there was no going back.

The ideas I had about love—for instance, that pure and true romantic love was the only love that really mattered—were not unusual; it wasn't like my mom and I sat in a dark cave espousing some kind of cultlike ideology about marriage. When I was growing up, those ideas were *everywhere*. The years between 1996 and 2008—my formative ones—were the highest-grossing box office years for romantic comedies in history.[8] The top five performing rom-com feature films came out before I was old enough to be legally married.

I recently rewatched "When Harry Met Sally."
I remembered it being REALLY GOOD.

it's fine.

Her orgasm-in-the-restaurant scene holds up.

BUT

His whole notion that men & women can't really be friends is so SAD.

If they were ME & MR. RORY, we'd end up platonic roommates.

I formed my ideas about love based on this version of relationships: meet, fall in love, get married (a white dress and a big ring are, importantly, involved in this step), maybe have a kid or two, and live happily ever after. But relationships have been changing. Over the past decade, more and more people have been raising children without being married or having a partner, and more and more women have decided not to have children at all.[9]

It extends to teenagers, too, in case you haven't noticed. The overarching trend in teen dating is this: teens today are doing less of it. In 2002, just 34.4 percent of tenth-graders reported that they "never date"; in 2013, that number had jumped up to 44 percent. It's possible that the definition of the word "date" is different than the definition of the term "hook up"; that social media has awakened more young people to the dangers of sex and dating; or that the kids of today are enjoying what Amy Davidson of *The New Yorker* calls "the extension of childhood."[10] In any case, I would be remiss not to state that there is a very real possibility that today's girls are less interested in being a girlfriend than I ever was.

And for the record, even my mom's ideas about love have changed. When I told her I was writing a book about polyamory, she was encouraging. Over ramen last Christmas, she began schooling *me* about the nomenclature of love.

I only recently started to consider the notion that I might not really know that much about her marriage. Forty-eight years is a *long time* to be in one relationship. My parents are both pretty mum about whether they've always been 100 percent technically monogamous. People do all kinds of things to make their relationships work, and a lot of it usually goes unspoken. Love is a sacrifice regardless of the form it takes. I don't know all the details of my parents' marriage, but I do know that they decided to stick it out with each other, and that when something awful happens—when a person in their lives gets sick or dies or hurts them—they don't have to face it alone. My dad makes scrambled eggs or pancakes on Sunday mornings, and they sit with a pair of pencils over the *New York Times* crossword puzzle and work through it with a calculated methodology that belongs only to them.

In the past decade, though, my mother has drastically changed her tune about the relationships in my life. Lately, she's been very careful to tell me that "It's okay if you don't want to get married. People don't have to get married anymore." She's happy in her marriage, and her marriage has lasted almost fifty years. And no matter what path I take—no matter how I ultimately choose to love—I'll still wonder what would have happened had I done it differently. My daughter (I hope I have a daughter) will, I imagine, wonder if there is yet another way to love.

Now, when I watch the birds outside my window (where I dangle my bird feeders, my binoculars always within reach), I picture them nesting on a tall branch far away, loving each other and raising their young together, and having sexual rendezvous with the neighbors when things are calm enough. Birds probably don't do that, either; birds operate in ways that humans will never be able to understand, which is part of what I love so much about them.

♡ ⌒ ♡ ⌒ ♡

But before I'd found any of this peace of mind having to do with love or birds or my parents or happily-ever-after, I had entered stage two of Project Perfect Boyfriend, and we were college bound. I was afraid to go to college. I woke up almost every night from awful dreams in which my classmates were shiny green aliens who couldn't understand the way I talked. Ben's parents had grown to really like me; his mom called one day to tell me she thought Ben would flounder if he didn't get some "cooler clothes" for college, and if she gave me some money, would I take him shopping? I thought this was a great idea; I wanted my college boyfriend to at least appear somewhat put-together.

We went to a hip second hand shop where they seemingly only buy clothes from people who used to be in semi successful bands.

WOOL PEACOAT WITH VINTAGE BUTTONS

Ben had grown out his hair to be "normal" brown.

SOMETHING FLANNEL

PINAFORE?

JEANS WITH STRATEGIC AMOUNTS OF HOUSE PAINT ON THEM

Months in advance, we were mailed our roommate assignments. I had been put with a girl whose French manicure was visible in her photograph, and whose cheeks were polished, apparently, with the dew from angels' wings. If this was what I was up against in college, I was doomed. Before we left in separate cars to begin our young adult lives, Ben bought a $50 pair of (nonpleated) jeans, and I had my hair dyed blond and cut like Mandy Moore's. (At least, I brought Mandy

Moore's picture in to the stylist; no one ever told me I even remotely resembled her after the fact.)

I figured that this time around, I would be the kind of girlfriend I always knew I could be.

PART 2

"Just" "Friends"

My mom wouldn't let me buy "Best Friends" jewelry. This was a major blow. Claire's sold such a lavish array of broken-heart pieces, matching pandas, and rhinestone-embedded word splices, and having "Best Friends" jewelry was essential to a person's popularity. At the mall, I would run my fingers longingly across the matching-set jewelry. It didn't even matter who had the other half of the necklace—having one indicated something very important to the rest of the world: that you were someone's favorite.

This was exactly my mother's objection. "No one really has just one best friend," she told me. "To pretend you do is to play a favorites game that leaves other people out."

"In the hierarchy of relationships," writes Julie Beck for *The Atlantic*, "friendships are at the bottom."[1] This is reflected everywhere from my mom's taste in jewelry to the little data available on the subject: while relationship science is rich, it tends to focus on the romantic definition of the word "relationship" and never (seriously—*never*) the platonic one. Popular media is also myopically focused on romantic love: movies about relationships almost unanimously center on romance; popular music about friendship essentially begins and ends with Randy Newman;[2] even the pivotal television show about what it means to be *Friends* deteriorates into a meditation on who's sleeping with whom, and ultimately dissolves as soon as the once-unhappy singles are happily coupled off.

It wasn't always this way. Aristotle, for one, disagreed, explaining that *philia* (often translated to "brotherly love," or, for our purposes, nonromantic love) is one of the highest forms of love. (Love, for those who skipped Plato's *Symposium*, was literally a godlike "great spirit" to the Ancient Greeks.)[3] He examines the three types of friendship in book VIII of *Nicomachean Ethics*: friendship based on utility (like when your boss invites you out for drinks, and you kind of *have* to get along because you both need each other), friendship based on pleasure (like when you have a one-night stand with the hot barista because she thinks you're hot, too), and then that really good sort of friendship that practically defies explanation. Aristotle describes this as a "complete sort of friendship between people who are good and alike in virtue." It comes from being good, finding someone else who is good, and loving, unsuperficially, the goodness in each other.

There are also plenty of what have been called "romantic friendships" in Victorian literature. Extremely intimate but nonsexual relationships between friends—sometimes involving holding hands, cuddling, hugging, kissing, or sharing a bed—are rife in the pages of books and letters by Charles Dickens, Charlotte Brontë, and Jane Austen. William Shakespeare ambiguously addressed 126 of his love sonnets to an adolescent boy,[4] which signified either his bisexuality or a deeply intense male friendship. The relationship might actually have fallen somewhere in the middle. Between the platonic and the sexual is a natural but ambiguous type of love between friends that seems to make contemporary Western societies uncomfortable. Today, the idea of a woman spending the night in the same bed with her best female friend and holding her close to her body—and maybe kissing her good night—is so strange that we can't hear about it without assuming something sexual (or at least kind of weird) is going on. For Brontë and Austen, such a physical female friendship was par for the course.

The general consensus about why friendship dies as we age is this: over time, life gets busier, people build families, and friends move away. The largest drop-off in friendship unsurprisingly tends to happen when people get married. Maybe it's because everyone (at least according to *my* Facebook feed) is always marrying their "best friends."

I don't get this. No matter how great the person is who's on your joint insurance plan—no matter how many things you share, how much you can laugh together, and how many shows Netflix designates as "couples' shows" for you—no one can be everything for anyone. That's a bitter pill to swallow. For years I drank all the Soul Mate Kool-Aid I could get my hands on; it's certainly seductive to believe that someone out there is made specifically for you.

I started to change my mind about that when Ben and I broke up. This happened on a Tuesday during our freshman year of college, while we sat in a park by a duck pond that smelled vaguely like sulfur. There had been a slow build to it. We lived in different residence halls, and there were way more cute boys in my residence hall than I thought there would be, and while I really loved Ben, I also really, really wanted to kiss the new cute boys. I didn't phrase it exactly that way when I broke up with him, though. The for-Ben version went something like: "We have to focus on our studies! And meet new people and do things! And not be distracted! But we're going to be friends forever, I promise, and this is ultimately going to be good, and we'll probably get back together really soon." Ben wasn't horrified, but he was cautious. Um, didn't I think that we belonged together? he wanted to know. Of course we belong together! I assured him.

This breakup was not all that dramatic, and, surprisingly, we *did* stay friends. Ben took me to buy lemon cake and get a tattoo when I went through a breakup with my next boyfriend. We moved in together during our junior year, and I brought home people I wanted to sleep with, and he brought home people he wanted to sleep with. I'm sure there were moments early on when we were both jealous, but my memories of college are filled with late nights playing Super Smash

Brothers in the living room, afternoons DJing at the college radio station, and making experimental chocolate-cherry cupcakes, and doing all of it with Ben.

I know that having this kind of friendship with an ex is uncommon. Friendships with exes, if attempted at all, often fail.[5] And while staying friend*ly* with an ex isn't especially rare (as in, you don't make voodoo dolls or anything, and you hug each other if you both have to go to a mutual friend's wedding), dubbing an ex your bestie is all but unheard-of.

According to social scientists, there are a few indicators that your failed romantic relationship might transition into a successful platonic one. If a relationship ends on a positive, amicable note, for example, your chances of staying friends are significantly higher.[6] A longstanding friendship preceding a romantic relationship—as Ben and I had in high school—also bodes well.[7] But what matters the most is how invested, committed, and satisfied each person in a romantic relationship is. The more a person is happy with her partner—the more she says she cares—the more likely it is that she'll maintain a healthy friendship with that partner after the romantic relationship has ended. I know—this totally goes against that whole "If we're not passionately fighting all the time, the fire just isn't there" stereotype you may have grown up believing. In truth, there are some ways in which relationships don't change all that much after the people in them stop kissing each other. Real love isn't easy to stamp out; you hold on to your affection even after you stop wanting to have sex.

After we graduated, Ben moved back to Portland, into a fratty house with a bunch of dudes. The house contained no fewer than nine video game consoles; the sink was always teeming with wet pizza crusts and plastic plates caked in crusted-over macaroni and cheese; and the sofa smelled like weed in a way that would never come out. I moved to New Orleans to be a teacher. Ben's parents, whom I remained close with, approved of my decision—they even took me out for Thai food. For a while, Ben was an unhappy actuary (which is perhaps redundant). I hated teaching. When I visited over Christmas, we sat across a slice of fudge cake at a diner as the tinny ceiling speakers wheezed out "Ave Maria" on the radio. We were both sadder than we knew how to explain. We sat in silence, Ben pushing a lump of cake around the plate with his fork, me drawing circles in ballpoint pen on a crumpled paper napkin.

And then, only a few weeks after that, Ben met Jen. Jen was young (she was eighteen, he was twenty-four), but she didn't seem young. They went on a few dates. For a while, Jen—who lived an hour or so away—drove to Portland, and they sat in Ben's living room and did jigsaw puzzles while it rained outside. They started dating more regularly. They fell in love. They moved together to Austin, where they adopted two cats and then a dog. They moved into a house that had a yard, and after Jen had to have hip surgery (twice), they decided there was no way they could live without each other.

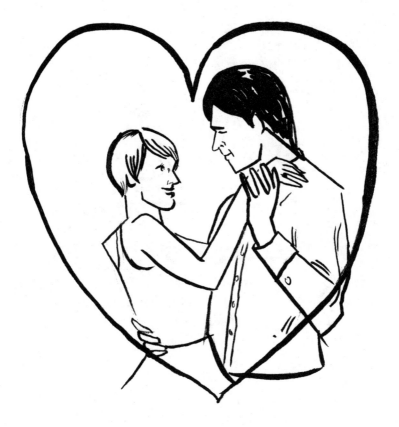

One winter, years later, I lay on the floor of the Portland airport trying to stretch out my back before my flight home to New Orleans. Leaving Portland after Christmas was always difficult. Ben didn't go to Portland every Christmas like I did; he and Jen split their family time. There was no way to go to Portland and not think of Ben, and I was used to that: I drove past the twenty-four-hour pie shop across the street from the movie theater where we once spent most Friday nights, and wondered which kids sat in the booths now; did they play cards at the table like we did, and did they dip their french fries in ice cream? Ben and I called each other on birthdays and holidays, and occasionally on long drives. I visited them (Ben and Jen were a package deal now) in Austin sometimes, and they visited me in New Orleans sometimes. While I was on the floor of the airport, Ben returned my yearly holiday call. I had to shout over the monotonous blare of departure times.

I thought, "I have never felt happier for any person, ever—maybe not even myself." I said, "Congratulations! Tell me everything!" And he told me everything, and two weeks later, under a quiet tree, she said yes.

It feels good to love someone enough to fully let go into the nature of a changing relationship. I felt—and continue to feel—proud of the friendship Ben and I share. I wish it hadn't taken an unusually positive experience with an ex to teach me how great friendship can be, but it did. The love I feel for Ben is more than friendship but less than romantic. It occupies a weird middle space that I would have completely overlooked had it not been for his patience and willingness to explore a different kind of relationship with me. Learning to prioritize friendship with Ben was ultimately the catalyst that led me to understand how I could begin to love women. And understanding how to love women—physically and emotionally—is the single greatest gift I've received during my time on earth so far.

I feel a little queasy writing "understanding how to love women" here. It seems like it should be an obvious thing, something animal and natural to anyone with a working sensibility. But remember: I'd come to believe that boyfriends and husbands were all that mattered. Life was a search for The One, and he would be a man, and when you found him, you locked him down. Even though I sometimes felt attracted to women, I rejected those feelings because women couldn't be husbands. Now, though, my entire relationship structure orbits around my love for women and the ways in which I've decided to prioritize my female friendships.

I need to mention here that the polyamory movement as it exists today owes a lot to queer culture. Where heterosexual couples have prioritized the so-called standard narrative (one man, one woman, one love, maybe a few kids), queer folks have experimented with relationship models for decades. As Susan Song puts it in a paper on polyamory and queer anarchism, "Queer theory resists heteronormativity and recognizes the limits of identity politics. The term 'queer' implies resistance to the 'normal,' where 'normal' is what seems natural and intrinsic."[8] An entire book could be written (and, actually, several *have* been written) on the connection between queer culture and polyamory. Polyamory is nothing new; it's been in and out of favor (under different names) since—well, probably since humanity itself. But the most recent iteration, which this book is mostly about, is a concept sculpted and cemented by queer folks all over the world.

For instance, Robin Bauer, a female-to-male transsexual, coproduced the first international conference on polyamory in 2005. In Deborah Anapol's words (she translated some of Bauer's lecture from its original German), "gay men have been practicing nonmonogamy from the get-go and consider heterosexuals to be Johnny-come-latelies."[9] And then there's Andie Nordgren, the gender-queer artist who invented the term "relationship anarchy" in 2006. In the first few lines of Nordgren's pamphlet *The Short Instructional Manifesto for Relationship Anarchy*, relationship anarchy sounds a lot like the version of polyamory I want to build my life around: "Relationship anarchy questions the idea that love is a limited resource that can only be real if restricted to a couple. You have capacity to love more than one person, and one relationship and the love felt for that person does not diminish love felt for another."[10] Relationship anarchy embraces ideas around spontaneity, freedom, respect, values, and a rejection of possession and entitlement. The term is gaining traction.

A friend recently sent me a comic from the website Feministing called "5 Radical Ways People Do Non-Monogamy That You Need to Know About." The comic features gender-queer people in three-way relationships, as well as people who are a-romantic (not interested in kissing or sex) but are in loving, lifelong relationships with multiple people. It's a comic I wish I had seen ten years ago, when I started to feel confused about where women fit in my love life. My best friends— Jessica is a great example—are almost always women, and while I usually don't have sex with them, our relationships are often even more intimate than my boyfriend-girlfriend relationships with men.

There's a page in a diary I kept in 2000 (this was pre-Ben) that attempts to chart the people I'd loved and the degree to which they broke my heart. The picture looks like this:

At that point, I'd never been physically intimate with a girl (unless you count Kate from my theater troupe, whom I kissed on the lips à la Katy Perry on a dare), but I had definitely loved girls. I remember drawing this chart and thinking, "Should the girls go in a different category?" And then, "No, all these people hurt me in the same kind of way." I was fourteen and had never dated anyone before, but I had had romantic crushes only on male-bodied people. The girls who had broken my heart had been my friends. This was the moment I should have realized that the one-man-one-woman-two-kids-together-forever relationship model wasn't quite right for me.

Long after Ben and I had dated and broken up, I followed a girl to Chicago. Beatrice had been my first friend in college, and we'd had a sort of slow, quiet falling out over the course of sophomore year. She'd moved into an on-campus house for community service, and I'd moved into one for global awareness. The Community Service House had house dinners together most nights and participated in a ton of service projects—volunteering at local elementary schools, painting fences, that kind of thing—that I was way too self-interested and egotistical to participate in. Beatrice and I saw less and less of each other until our time together dwindled to one Friday-afternoon lunch date in the campus center every month and a half or so.

I missed Beatrice. When we'd met freshman year, we thrift-shopped and primped for the '80s-themed dance together. On Halloween, we wore matching *Newsies* costumes and took hundreds of pictures in every pose we could think of with the digital camera my grandfather had given me as a graduation present. We lay on Beatrice's roommate's loft bed and talked about the boys we had crushes on and made plans to seduce them.

Once we began *actually* seducing the boys—and getting into long-term relationships with them—there was (surprise!) considerably less time to spend with each other. I'll bear the brunt of the responsibility for the drop-off in our friendship; my feelings about Finding The One had not matured much since high school.

Months after we stopped hanging out regularly, Beatrice told me that she had decided to spend her first semester of junior year in Chicago. The school we went to was renowned for its rich study-abroad program. Studying abroad had never appealed to me, because I liked to be able to order Pizza Hut and get Taco Bell whenever I wanted. It would probably be okay for a week or so, but what would I do a week in when I got a craving for something made entirely out of chemicals and everyone around me spoke only Japanese? Plus, what about Thanksgiving? Thanksgiving was reserved for American overeaters and football watchers. If I was in another country, I would miss Thanksgiving, and I worried that would give me a panic attack.

I hadn't considered studying in another city in the United States, though. Beatrice told me there were two programs that allowed you to study domestically at our school—one in Chicago and one in Philadelphia. They were "urban studies" programs—a term Beatrice knew all about because she was a sociology major. I didn't know what sociology was, and I had never heard the word "urban" next to a word that wasn't "outfitters." But as an English major, I knew quite a lot about Geoffrey Chaucer. I rationalized that at least Chaucer and Chicago both started with the same digraph, so it wasn't unreasonable to think that a semester in the Windy City might be good for me, too. Plus, I really missed Beatrice.

Probably they have Pizza Hut in Chicago.

I wanted to see if I could salvage my friendship with her. At the time, I was in a pretty unhealthy relationship with a man (he's one of the few in my pictorial timeline with a fake name and an invisible face, because we're not on good terms); I secretly wanted some time away from him. And so, without consulting her (or my boyfriend) about it first, I followed Beatrice to Chicago.

The term started in the fall; there was a long, sticky summer to read packets of papers and spiral-bound primers about the city and the potential neighborhoods you could live in. I was placed in Hyde Park, which houses the University of Chicago, a gigantic and prestigious university that's hard to get into and produces famous people like Philip Glass, Roger Ebert, Kurt Vonnegut, and David Rockefeller. The only real way to get from Hyde Park to anywhere else in the city is to take the no. 6 bus, which follows an express route along the highway past the Field Museum and into the Loop. From there you can ride trains to places like Logan Square or Ravenswood, but you'd be talking about commutes of over an hour—longer if it's rush hour, and it's rush hour 50 percent of the time in Chicago. The students in my urban studies program who were headquartered in Hyde Park mostly stayed in Hyde Park, and I was no exception.

I mention this because Beatrice was *not* placed in Hyde Park—she was much farther north, and I saw her only once a week or so when the whole cohort gathered for classes. I spent my time with my Hyde Park roommates—Lia, Bruno, and Trent. There were other groups of roommates in the program who lived in Hyde Park, too, and I slowly got to know them. There was Kitten, a runner who insisted everyone call her Kitten and never Kit; and there was Jasmine, who wouldn't eat anything made with corn syrup. There were also three girls who all went to Villanova and had blond hair and refused to do anything without one another. And then there was Kim.

Kim wore her hair in a chin-length bob; she had a thick fringe of bangs along her forehead, and the day we met she wore a lime-green pencil skirt. Her eyes were enormous and brown and impossible to look away from. She had a car, and she volunteered to drive me downtown once when the Hyde Park kids all went to the Pancake House for breakfast on a school day. I sat in the front seat of her car, and she popped a Belle and Sebastian CD into the player. She kept a stack of silver mix CDs in her console, and I thumbed through them as we drove—some had Sharpie hearts drawn on them, or little messages that suggested nothing about what songs they might hold ("I Believe in You"). I thought Belle and Sebastian was a fairly basic band, and my immediate reaction to being in a car with *The Boy with the Arab Strap* blasting out of the tinny speakers was to feel hubristic about how unique and alternative my own taste in music was.

Neither of us immediately recognized our compatibility; I'm not great at judging people, and I also don't make that good a first impression, so I guess that was no surprise. But Kim almost instantly caught the attention of my roommate Trent, who was a traditionally good-looking guy with stupid-bright eyes. (I'm talking about the kind of eyes that another person might describe as "piercing.") Kim and Trent hit it off right away.

This was lucky, because Kim started to hang out at my apartment to spend time with Trent. (I maybe should have emphasized more that Kim looks like a supermodel. She's Chilean, with a creamy butterscotch complexion; she's also a dancer, and she moves like one. People fall in love with her at first sight a *lot*.) When she wasn't around, Trent talked to me about how enamored with Kim he was, and how irritating it was that she had a long-distance boyfriend. Then, one Friday night, there was a party in Logan Square. I hated parties (I guess I'd never been to one, really, but I assumed that I hated them, because I wanted to be the kind of person who hated parties), and I'd seen in the *Chicago Reader* that M. Ward was playing that night at the Metro, a club uptown. (See how alternative my musical taste was? M. Ward! Who my age had even *heard* of M. Ward at that point? None of my roommates, that's for sure.) I decided to go to the concert; my roommates went to the party.

That Saturday, Kim was in our apartment lounging on the couch and thumbing through one of Trent's magazines and she asked me why I hadn't been at the party.

This was when I realized that I'd sold Kim short. Not only did she know who (the very alternative) M. Ward was, she had known that he was playing last night. I considered the lime-green pencil skirt she had had on when we met. It was a pretty bold skirt; a cool move for a person who could wear a pair of sweatpants and look like she had stepped out of a Victoria's Secret catalog.

Kim and I started hanging out in our classes. We collaborated on a video project about the assets of Hyde Park. We decided to write a dark, moody rap song and layer it on top of video footage of the neighborhood. (It's still on YouTube—it's called "Hyde Park Assets." That video contains several hallmarks: the first time either of us used a digital video camera; the first time we ever uploaded anything to YouTube; and the first time we played with Garage Band—hence the cringe-worthy overuse of drum kit samples.) I went to her house, and we made epic dance-party playlists on iTunes and then danced to them in her living room. We stayed home from parties to have sleepovers and order Domino's. It wasn't long before Kim had completely stopped coming to our apartment to visit Trent; now she came to see me.

Things only intensified. We both had long-distance boyfriends, but we found ourselves talking to them less so we could spend more time with each other. We were together most nights. When we walked around Chicago, we held hands. Once, we went to Andersonville and decided to pretend like we were on our first date. We leaned in toward each other over a Mediterranean dinner and asked each other first-date questions as though we were ourselves from the future.

And then I thought about how she wore her hair with bangs. I hadn't thought about it much until that moment, but I decided that bangs were definitely trendy, and that, in fact, I would have to cut bangs for my hair, too. I noticed, also, that she had a little heart tattooed on her ankle. She was the first person I knew in real life with a tattoo. It was suddenly undeniable: Kim was cool. I'd been so focused on winning back Beatrice's affection that I hadn't really been paying attention to the other people in the program.

I thought about Kim a lot. It wasn't the kind of pelvic, *Hustler* sort of thinking that I often engaged in when I had boy crushes, but it was just as consistent and vibrant. I imagined living with Kim in a dusty house on the periphery of Chicago. I pictured having fat cats with her. In my fantasy, our boyfriends lived with us, too, but they were sort of on the sidelines, going to work constantly and staying out late with the guys. In real life, we said "I love you"—we even wrote poetry for each other—but I don't think either of us recognized the love as romantic.

Eventually, the program ended, and we both moved back to our respective college towns. We spoke on the phone every Sunday afternoon for a while; I visited Kim at her school, and she visited me at mine; during a joint vacation in Portland we got matching tattoos of pigeon silhouettes. It was an accidentally serious long-distance relationship. And then, as is common in long-distance relationships, our separate lives got very busy, and time lapsed longer between calls.

Friendships change differently than romantic relationships; they have an elasticity that romantic relationships don't. It's rarer for friendships to end in breakups; rather, they tend to shrink and swell as time and space allow. I still visit Kim in Los Angeles about once a year. This year it was just for an hour—I was in town for a conference, and we grabbed lunch at a crowded food-cart garage full of loud men in tight jeans and waifish women in shorts that looked like underpants. The hour was enough; with deep friendships like that, sometimes an hour is all you need.

On a recent phone call, Kim—who was starting to experiment with the concept of polyamory inside her six-year relationship—told me that she was interested in dating women. And then she said, "You were the first girl I ever dated. I mean, I realized recently that when we lived in Chicago, we were dating. We were in love with each other and we were dating; we just didn't have sex or anything." She said this so simply and matter-of-factly that I couldn't believe I hadn't seen it myself. But it was more than that, too; this was another landmark turning point in my understanding of love. When Ben and I broke up but stayed friends, I began to see love as something outside romance. With Kim, the revelation was equal and opposite: we were "friends"—a term I had a loose understanding of—but there was somehow more to it than that. We didn't get physical, but I prioritized her more than I had prioritized friends in the past. As in my relationship with Ben post-breakup, I didn't have terms or parameters to define how I felt about Kim—and it was exciting. To this day, I wonder what our relationship could have become if we had had longer than a semester in Chicago to explore it.

Which brings me to Hannah Sadtler.

I met Hannah two years after I met Kim. I want to say this outright: the love I cultivated with Hannah is, without a doubt in my mind, the greatest love of my life so far. If I believed in God or otherworldly powers (and some days, depending on my mood and how hormonal I am, I do), Hannah would be my reason for doing so.

We met in an airport. We were flying to Arizona, where we were both going to a summerlong training session for new teachers; she recognized me from a preliminary session we'd attended earlier that week. I was attracted to her in a way that's difficult to describe. It wasn't a romantic crush, exactly, but my stomach lurched when she spoke to me, sort of like the way it did when I was going to give a speech in front of a full auditorium.

She asked me thoughtful questions about the Pacific Northwest—what I enjoyed doing on the weekends and how I felt about suddenly living in a place that was so hot and swampy. She'd recently spent some time living and working on a farm, and hoped that she would have enough time to keep making squash soup after she started teaching.

I found myself hanging on her words; her company was familiar and warm. She laughed effortlessly and made eye contact; she brushed my shoulder with her hand purposefully when she responded to me. I was scared of her.

In the past, I've used the word "intimidating" to describe this quality in women. Now I don't think that word is quite right. "Intimidating" is a word I use to shift focus away from myself; if Hannah is "intimidating," then I'm not to blame for being scared of her. But to describe someone like Hannah as intimidating is to do her—and women in general—a disservice.

While I was studying in Arizona, I saw Hannah on campus frequently. I was so uncomfortably infatuated with her that when I saw her coming, I crossed the street to walk on the opposite sidewalk so we wouldn't have to interact. She waved to me in the cafeteria, and I responded with chilly half smiles. Eventually, I noticed that she was spending most of her free time with two attractive girls who I could tell were much cooler than I was. "Of course," I thought. "Those are the girls she's meant to be friends with." I grew comfortable with the story that Hannah had rejected me in favor of those cooler girls.

Another girl, Leah, was much more aggressive about being friends with me, and although I felt she was too cool for me, too (can you sense a theme here?), she called a lot and insisted that we "hang out." We were both vegans, and she had a car, so she took me to vegan restaurants in Phoenix (few and far between, but you don't complain when you're a vegan) at least once a week. Leah had also met Hannah, but she had not been intimidated, and they'd become friends. Over dinner, I told Leah that I thought Hannah was cold and dismissive. "What? No way," Leah said. "You just have to spend a little more time with her."

Later I learned that Hannah had, likewise, thought I was cold and dismissive. (In fairness, this was probably because I had acted cold and dismissive.) After we'd all finished the teacher training and were back in New Orleans, Hannah and I ended up at the same party at Leah's house. I remember the party because it fell on the same day that my long-distance boyfriend, Sean, broke up with me. Hannah remembers the party because near its end, I (extremely drunkenly) told her that I was good at cutting hair, and that she had beautiful hair. Hannah needed a haircut, so this was useful information.

Hannah came over on a Saturday afternoon in October. We sat in the courtyard at the house I had rented in Uptown, and I cut her hair with children's craft scissors. Just as it had in the airport when we met, conversation with Hannah came easily. She volleyed questions and answered mine with graceful equilibrium. Her hair—which was very shiny and stick-straight—was unforgiving in the hands of a novice stylist, though, and the uneven chunks I left were impossible to ignore.

When she saw her new haircut—which really did look like a kid's multimedia art project—in the mirror, she (quite generously) said, "I love it. It's edgy!" We swept up what we could, although a film of hair remained on the sweaty bricks for weeks afterward, stubbornly clinging to that lovely afternoon.

In January of our first year teaching, Leah and I threw Hannah a birthday party. By then, the three of us had developed an enviable friendship; we had chatty weekly dinners and talked on the phone about our miserable jobs. Leah and I decided to surprise Hannah after work by hanging streamers and balloons all over her house. Leah was an exceptional baker, and she crafted an artisanal cayenne-chocolate cake, complete with complex piping up the sides. Hannah was stunned when she saw it all; she practically choked up, mumbling something about how having good friends made hard situations easier.

She invited people over for a potluck brunch. Potlucks were a beloved part of the twentysomething experience, and there seemed to be one every week, which was okay, because otherwise no one would eat anything that didn't come in a box. Hannah was dating a guy she had gone out with a few times, but she didn't seem all that invested in him. He came to the potluck; she kept jumping up to tend to the napkins or to refill the water glasses whenever he reached for her arm. There was another guy there, though, who made her laugh, and who climbed the street sign outside while everyone else ate scones on the porch. That guy's name was Derek, and within a year he and Hannah would be kissing for the first time in the triangular park just off the bayou. It was 2009; we'd all been out of college and living in New Orleans for almost a year. A few months later, Derek and Hannah moved in together. And I moved in with them.

Research shows that one of the keys to lasting relationships tends to be proximity—hence all the ill-fated long-distance romances that fall apart despite everyone's excellent intentions. Living with Hannah brought us together all the time—at least twice a day, when we poked around the kitchen making meals. I have a theory that cook-at-home-together people are closer than people who go out to eat. There's something about boiling potatoes in your underwear while rummaging through the freezer for some rogue pecans that's more honest than sitting in a party dress at a five-star ramen place.

At some point after we moved in together, I thought I must be in love with Hannah. I wanted to be around her all the time, and I thought about her while I was on vacation looking at desert rocks or national monuments. Every morning we embraced while the water was boiling for coffee and the cast iron was heating up for eggs. Sometimes when I couldn't sleep, I thought about how in the morning I would get to hug my best friend, and I reminded myself that I was not really alone.

Three years after they started dating, Hannah and Derek opened up their relationship. The shift was mostly theoretical. They were allowed to pursue other people if they wanted to, or kiss without consequence on Mardi Gras. (Everyone should be able to kiss without consequence on Mardi Gras. Whether or not secret kissing is cheating, I consider this inarguable.) With a few fleeting exceptions, though, they didn't date other people. What they did do was sleep in separate rooms.

Hannah liked to go to bed late; her task-riddled anxiety swept her up into the night. Derek liked to get up early; he was stalwart about practicing meditation and liked to do it at the traditional crack of dawn. They wanted to decorate their rooms differently. And maybe more than anything, they sometimes needed space.

In my twenties, the person who felt most "made for me" was Hannah. My friendship with her was the first friendship I had wherein I felt we were both equally committed to learning the balance. For the first time in my life, I was totally comfortable around another person; I didn't feel the need to dress anything up. For instance, I told Hannah that I'd always faked my orgasms, which I'd never told anyone before. I told her because I knew she would be able to hear it and not reject me for it; I knew she would give me her time and her patience and her honest opinion. (Her honest opinion, of course, was that it was much better to not fake orgasms. But she also helped me dig into the reasons why I faked them.)

Another time, Hannah heard me crying in my room. She softly knocked at the door, asking if she could come in. Had it been any other person, I would have said no, or I would have said nothing, or I would have left the house. But it was Hannah. She came in and sat on my bed, and without saying another word, she wrapped her arms around me, and I felt safe. It was my friendship with Hannah that paved the way for every relationship that came after. I felt—and there is no better term for this—in love with her.

But Hannah had a partner. And more than that, I liked that she had a partner, and I liked her partner—I even *loved* her partner; and as much as I loved them both, I didn't want to have sex with either of them. I wanted to have sex with the clarinet player from the street parades, but I didn't want to live with him. I liked going to the movies and cuddling up next to the comic-book artist I dated in New Orleans, and making out with him was the best (he did this barely-touching-soft-lips thing that I thought happened only on *Dawson's Creek*), but I didn't want to lie in bed with him on Sunday mornings.

♡ 〜 ♡ 〜 ♡

The trouble with the way my peers often use the word "polyamory" is that there tends to be too much emphasis on sex. In some of my social circles, "polyamory" and "hookup culture" are synonymous. In my personal experience, the two couldn't be farther apart. Aren't there relationships that fall somewhere between platonic and nonplatonic? Isn't there love that exists beyond "friendship" and outside of "lover" and paradoxically both inside and outside of "family"?

In his essay "For Lovers and Fighters," Dean Spade writes that one of his goals in being polyamorous is to treat his lovers more like his friends, and his friends more like his lovers. One of the problems with dating just one person is that he sees "people prioritizing romantic relationships over all else—ditching their friends, putting all their emotional eggs in one basket, and creating unhealthy dynamics with the people they date because of it. It becomes simultaneously the most important relationship and the one where people act out of their most insecure selves."[11]

When I began to explore what polyamory would mean for me, it had everything to do with my relationship with Hannah. For much of the time that I lived in New Orleans, I needed a way to explain that my most significant relationship was with a woman I was not sleeping with, and that I was open to other (sexual and nonsexual) relationships, too. This felt familiar; it reminded me of how I felt about Kim when we both lived in Chicago. Had you asked me then who the most important person in my life was, I wouldn't have batted an eyelash before saying that it was Kim. Now, with Hannah, I hoped I could finally put words to this priority. I wanted to define polyamory on my own terms: I didn't have any interest in a "primary" partner. (Many people in polyamorous relationship structures identify one person as their "primary" and all subsequent relationships as "secondary" or "tertiary.") I needed the people I slept with to understand that Hannah was one of my biggest priorities. I wanted a definition of the word polyamory that embraced all of this at once.

Luckily for me, Deborah Anapol gives us just that: "The freedom of surrendering to love and allowing love—not just sexual passion, not just social norms and religious strictures, not just emotional reactions and unconscious conditioning—to determine the shape our intimate relationships take is the essence of polyamory."[12] She adds that polyamory "involves a conscious decision to act altruistically, that is, to put the well-being of others on an equal par with one's own."[13] To me, that's what being a really good friend is all about. Polyamory is the continuation of the life we left behind when we hit puberty and, hypothetically, started searching for a singular perfect mate. It's the bringing-enough-cupcakes-for-the-whole-class deal: try to treat everyone with equal intention toward love, generosity, and respect, and see where it takes you.

On my thirtieth birthday, I had a quintessentially shitty day plagued with bad luck. The summer before, I'd moved from New Orleans to Chicago. It was my first year living away from Hannah and the friends I'd had for almost a decade. I felt very lonely, but I was determined to overcome this loneliness by planning activities for myself that I knew I would love. I tried to get pie at the new pie restaurant down the street (I love pie like it's my religion), but, tragically, the restaurant was closed. Then I tried to go bird-watching—as my birthday is gloriously in the middle of Chicago's warbler season—but it started to rain. (In

May? Unheard-of.) And then the guy who was going to give me my thirtieth-birthday tattoo—yes, I thought that undergoing a few hours of barely tolerable pain was a good way to celebrate my birth—told me I had fat arms! He meant it as a compliment (as in, "You have good, fat arms that will accommodate a tattoo like this well"), but come on: fat arms are never not the worst.

By 2:00 p.m. I had relegated myself to my bedroom, where I was sobbing into a bowl of stale tortilla chips.

A few days later, I went to New Orleans to visit Hannah. She picked me up in her maroon pickup truck and drove me to her house. When we got there, she opened the back door to a yard full of some of my oldest friends, all gathered around Derek, who was leading a sing-along. Tables had been covered in linen cloths and tall citronella candles to keep the bugs away; there were bowls of homemade salads and casseroles and guacamole; and there were multiple (MULTIPLE) kinds of fresh pie.

I should have known this would happen. I love birthdays—I think they're such wonderful opportunities to celebrate the people you love, people you so often forget to celebrate in the bedlam of scheduling crises and to-do lists. Hannah knows I love birthdays, and she wasn't going to let this one pass without something incredible happening; she never had before, so why should a thousand miles change anything? In our family (Hannah and Derek and I started calling each other "family" about five years ago), the cornerstone of any birthday celebration is the part where everyone sits in a circle and shares personal memories. They're sometimes funny and sometimes not. It's one of my favorite traditions.

During the memory circle for my surprise thirtieth birthday, Hannah talked about the time we went to Bogue Chitto State Park in Louisiana on a hundred-degree day. I remembered the day exactly—I'd been going through a work crisis that felt so terrible that I didn't know how I would ever feel better. It was too hot to think, too hot to cook. We thought about going tubing a few hours away, but that sounded like a commitment we didn't have the energy for, so we threw a heap of towels into my silver Volvo sedan and set out for the nearest, chilliest river we could think of. (Besides the Mississippi, which is visibly polluted, and has been rumored to cause people to grow extra limbs.)

When we reached the river, I parked under the only sliver of tree I could find, but it was way too skinny to produce anything like shade. The ground leading to the water was stony, with smooth rocks that pressed into your feet as you walked toward the river. The current was strong in places but mild in others; we waded in at a shallow spot that stretched a hundred yards across and was knee-deep in the middle. In the river, the white noise of water rushing over rocks drowned out the earsplitting screeches of midday cicadas—especially rowdy when the air was as hot and wet as it was that day—and in the icy quiet you could finally hear yourself think.

After a few minutes of acclimating, we agreed to float a little ways down the river, using our forearms to keep ourselves gently tethered to the ground. We reached a place where the water was deep, but a red maple had fallen across its narrow width. We both grabbed hold of the tree so we could stay in one place, tumbling like wind socks in the current.

By the time we fixed ourselves to the tree, Hannah and I had already spent three hours talking nonstop. The conversation rolled forward unpredictably. There were no lulls or awkward pauses; the things we wanted to say turned up without announcement, and then we broke off into other topics altogether.

Women are especially good at this, psychiatrists Jean Baker Miller and Irene Pierce Stiver point out: they engage in what Miller and Stiver call "connective" conversations—conversations that are uniquely healing, and, unfortunately, critically absent in public discourse. According to Miller and Stiver, connectivity occurs when both people engaged in a conversation are equally invested and share the emotional weight of the conversation's experience. "Connection in this sense does not depend upon whether the feelings are happy or sad or something else; it means having feelings *with* another person, aside from the specific nature of the feelings."[14]

Conversation with Hannah was long and easy because we were not necessarily seeking solutions to our problems. In discussing the pleasures and pains of our daily lives, we constructed reality together. I know this is convoluted and theoretical-sounding, so here's an example. Around the time of this trip, I was going through a particularly rough falling-out with a group of comedians I had been producing shows with for about a year and a half. In the car on the way to the river, Hannah—well acquainted with my fragile emotions on the subject—asked how I was doing in regard to the falling-out. She connected to me by relating my feelings to her own recent interactions with some coworkers. I've charted an example on the next page.

The focus on emotion rather than solution drives the conversation and allows things to come out that we may not have been expecting. In the example on the next page, Hannah was having some serious feelings about her relationship with coworker Rory and the ways in which Rory exploited Hannah's friendship in order to hurt Other Rory. That came up later, and the emotional space then shifted to fit Hannah's pain and frustration. This kind of conversation is hard to explain in words. Miller and Stiver spend 248 pages trying to do it in their book, and even then, they're hard-pressed to explain this kind

of conversation to people who don't regularly engage in it (read: most heterosexual cis-gendered men).

One of the things people seem to not be able to understand about connective conversations is why a person would want to engage in them if the conversation isn't going to solve any problems: "Our society tends to portray and value action as the result of the forceful exertion of the lone individual."[15] I guess this had a lot to do with my childhood belief that it was the job of a good girlfriend to swoop in and solve every problem.

Sometimes I don't need a solution nearly as much as I need to be told that whatever crazy thing I'm feeling—terrified of going to sleep at night; palpably angry at the bagel guy for working at an establishment that has run out of poppy-seed bagels; in love, unconditionally, with people who can't love me back—is an okay thing to feel. I'm constantly amazed at the ways in which our world seems to believe that uncomfortable feelings are abnormal and should be avoided or fixed at all costs. I've worked with counselors, therapists, psychiatrists, and spiritual mentors throughout my life. I've been on antidepressants and antianxiety medications for my particular brand of crazy. Hannah never tries to fix my problems; she sits with me in their shadows, engaging with the darkness until it passes.

At Bogue Chitto, as we floated in the river holding on to the tree branch, the water transformed into a gigantic, obvious metaphor, and both of us could feel it. Rivers—and the bits of detritus and schools of fish and hunks of rocks they carry—are inexorable. I mean, they all really go only one way: forward. Rivers don't make decisions, but they carve the earth like thoughtful sculptors; whether a tributary that swells over millions of years will curve to the west or to the east is anybody's guess, but rivers allow themselves to be carried forward inside the great mystery of time and space. Life is just like that: You have to allow yourself to be carried forward by its great mysteries, because they're going to come whether you want them to or not. All the pain and fear and love and struggle can be behind us only if we're brave enough to go through them.

And the only thing any of us really wants is to not have to go through it alone. We want the kind of love we can come back to after there's some turbulence and the current gets out of control. We want to look over and see that people are still there, were there all along, and will be there for the foreseeable future. Do you really need this love to look the way you thought it was going to look? Does it have to be a man, two kids, and a golden retriever?

Hannah was wise in bringing up our trip to the river in the memory circle, because really, it reflected our entire complicated relationship in as a succinct a way as was possible.

I should mention that things had changed in New Orleans when I visited just after my thirtieth birthday. Perhaps most relevant to my life (and to a book about polyamory), Hannah and Derek had dissolved their partnership a few months earlier. "Dissolved their partnership" sounds like a euphemism for "broke up," but they didn't break up. Derek moved out of the house, and they stopped planning their lives around each other. They still had the same long conversations they always did, just with less frequency. (Note how Derek was central to the Hannah-coordinated surprise birthday party thrown for me in the backyard.)

A little while into Hannah's foray into the single life, she started dating a woman. The woman, Ada, was a brilliant, soft-spoken film-maker who went to Harvard but never told anyone she went to Harvard. Ada wore rectangular plastic glasses and long cotton shirts over baggy jeans, and kept her hair cut short. This is the kind of uniform a person wears when he or she or they is so confident about themselves that they don't need to dress up their personality at all. Ada embodied everything I wished I was but felt too weak to be. I was terrified of her.

When Hannah told me over the phone that she had fallen in love with Ada, there was a butterfly migration inside my body—not liter-ally, but I can't describe the way it felt more accurately than to say that millions of butterflies that had been cocooned in my organs suddenly burst free. Deborah Anapol describes the feeling slightly better (and less horrifically): "love, sexual arousal, fear, and anger . . . blended together into one gigantic ball of energy that threatens to overwhelm the rational mind."[16] The other word Anapol uses for this kind of feeling is "jealousy."

It seemed impossible that I would feel so jealous in the face of my best friend's happiness. Didn't I want Hannah to have love in her life? Didn't I want her to experience all the woozy feelings that come during the honeymoon stage of a new relationship? I did. I wanted Hannah to win the lottery and roll around in a pit full of money before being named the empress of the universe. (Actually, Hannah would hate rolling around in money because she hates capitalism, and she wouldn't want to be the empress of the universe because she hates traditional power structures; so maybe I should say that I wanted Hannah to have unlimited raspberries and mangoes all the time until she died, and for her to have a three-way with her yoga instructor and bell hooks.)

But Hannah, the love of my adult life, was a person I'd known as always being coupled with a man. She and I shared a private sisterhood in which we knew all about periods and growing boobs and having childhood crushes on Jonathan Taylor Thomas, and Derek would never be able to fully enter that world. Now Hannah was with a woman. The tiny, selfish whisper inside my brain said, "That could have been you. Or maybe you're not good enough for her, anyway." Meanwhile, the tinier, altruistic whisper inside my brain said, "Hannah is happy, and if anyone can hold many different kinds of important relationships, it's her. This is great news. Celebrate!"

I will return to the subject of jealousy later (in some ways, I've found polyamory to be just as much about the personal exploration of jealousy as it is about exploring love or intimacy or friendship), but in this case, I realized that my relationship with Hannah was even more complicated than I had so far imagined.

Ada was at my surprise birthday party. During the memory circle, she said she didn't know that much about me, but she loved me for how much I loved Hannah. I wanted to hold her hands. I wanted to look her in the eyes and say, "The feeling is mutual."

PART 3

Casual Love

It's possible that you're thinking to yourself, "This is all very well and good, and I'm glad to be thinking about my friends and everything, but I thought I was going to read about *polyamory*. Which, I thought, had at least *something* to do with dating." Very astute, reader! Yes—to most people, the word "polyamory" stretches beyond finding a healthy balance between your friends and the people you're sleeping with.

Let's pause to consider a few terms that describe relationship models that tend to get tangled up in conversations about "modern love." The purpose of the chart on the next page is to differentiate these terms for the duration of this book, and to provide a framework that you might build your own definitions on.

These differences took me a long time to understand. When I started to think about trying nonmonogamy, it was because I was in my early twenties and thought I should "date around." I'd dated Eli and Ben (both long-term relationships that lasted a year and a half), and then an artist named Mac (for a year and a half), a vegan named Rory (for a year and a half), an improv comedian named Sean (for a year and change), a teacher named Rory (for the six months before he had to move), and a comic-book artist named Sam (for more than two years). I'd hopped from one long, dramatic, monogamous relationship to the next—usually without more than a week or so in the single lane. I was with Sam the longest, and that was the breakup that broke me.

Sam was, as I said, a comic-book artist. We met after I sent him a fan letter; his drawings of swampy forests and people sitting on buses

TERM	Polyamory	Open Relationships
ORIGINATED	Appeared in "Green Egg Magazine" in 1992	Has been recognized since the 1970s
IN A NUT-SHELL	The practice of individual relationships where individuals have more than one partner, with the knowledge & consent of all.	Relationship in which parties agree for any number of reasons to be in a non-monogamous relationship
FOR EXAMPLE	Three people living in a triad & loving each other. 	Rory & Roryette are in love, but Rory casually sleeps with men on the side.
DOES IT ALWAYS LOOK LIKE THAT?	Nope.	Nope.
COULD SIMULTANEOUSLY BE	·open relationship ·relationship anarchy	·polyamory ·casual sex ·relationship anarchy
KEY DIFF-ERENCE	knowledge, communication & consent	blanket term

TERM	Casual Sex	Relationship Anarchy
ORIGINATED	Began to be recognized in the 1920s	2010
IN A NUT-SHELL	A lifestyle that focuses on physical pleasure without emotional bonding or long-term commitment	Relationship model not bound by any set of rules
FOR EXAMPLE	Rory goes on a date with a new person every week. She sometimes has sex afterward.	Rory is asexual & lives with Rory II & Rory III, who occasionally have sex but sleep in separate rooms.
DOES IT ALWAYS LOOK LIKE THAT?	Nope.	Nope.
COULD SIMULTANEOUSLY BE	•open relationship •relationship anarchy	•polyamory •casual sex •open relationship
KEY DIFF-ERENCE	low commitment	no rules

were so beautiful that I replaced my desktop wallpaper immediately upon seeing them. It turned out that Sam and I had a mutual friend (thanks, Facebook!), and one New Year's Eve we ended up at the same party. I was moody (new years make me feel existential in the worst way) and he had a girlfriend at the time, but we hit it off nevertheless. That summer we were both in Portland and single, and after a week of dillydallying and saying a lot of variations of "I like you, but you live sooooo far away," we finally kissed while lying in the grassy shade of a public park. We both took off our glasses; I thought it was so cute to see them stacked one on top of the other.

We decided to give long distance a try, and it actually worked pretty well for us. Sam lived in Washington State, where he was finishing college; I taught first grade in New Orleans. We sent each other long emails every single night. (Yes, every single night—no exceptions. At one point, about a year in, I had our email correspondence printed and bound because I didn't trust the Internet to hold on to the lovely footprints of our early love.) Sam spent a summer with me in New Orleans; one year he worked at a sno-ball shop plopping sweetened condensed milk on syrupy ice before meeting me for dinner on our porch. We rendezvoused in Portland regularly, because our parents all lived there. We were able to see each other for a few days approximately once a month, and since we spent so much time outside of those days on the phone and composing our modern epistolary, that was enough.

Sam was younger than I was by four years, which is a lot when one is in one's early twenties. But I thought—no, I *knew*; I was constantly writing in my diary from that time that "I know that this is the real thing" and "In twenty years, once we've been married for a while . . ."—that our love was unique and permanent.

We had been together for two years when it was time to start thinking about where we would move after Sam graduated from college. I composed a fun list of multiple-choice questions for our future. I loved daydreaming about my future with Sam, who would be my husband, and with whom I would share a stupidly photogenic dog.

Choice one: Hip Brooklyn apartment.

Choice two: Beautiful outdoorsy Oregon.

Choice three: Fabulous, classic New Orleans

But, looking back, I realize that Sam never had the same enthusiasm about our future. It simply did not occur to me that I wasn't in his long-term plan; he told me every once in a while that he thought we'd probably get married, and that was enough for me: I began designing wedding invitations in my mind. (I pictured a letterpress drawing of glasses adorably stacked on top of each other. Once I put it on Pinterest, it would surely get pinned like a million times.) But in hindsight, I remember him saying other things, too: once over sweet-potato tacos he mentioned that we were at different stages in our lives. Another time he said he wanted to do a fellowship in Japan after college. I brushed all this off. When he broke up with me over the phone, I couldn't understand what he was saying. I felt like he was speaking another language, like he was carrying on in Swahili, even though I kept interrupting to implore him to speak in English. On and on in a language I couldn't understand, and then, "I'm sorry," and that was the end.

After the phone call, I walked to a Halloween party at a coworker's house, because that's what I had been planning to do and I couldn't think of an alternative. I had abstained from alcohol for three years because Sam didn't drink and I didn't find drinking enjoyable, but on this particular night, I gave that up—because what was the point?—and decided to drink an unmentionable number of vodka cranberries at the party. At first this went well, and everyone at the party thought I was a lot of fun. ("Everyone come in the living room! Sophie's doing impressions of Republican senators!") Then it was terrible, and I was sobbing uncontrollably, as though someone had uncorked a barrel inside me. And then my memory gets foggy. The things I remember are (1) the woman whose party it was let me lie in her bed and watch *Spice World*, which was miraculously on TBS that night; (2) I vomited on her comforter; and (3) someone at the party thought I should go to the hospital, and I kept repeating the same thing:

When I finally got through to them, Derek and Hannah drove across town to take me home. At this point, Derek and Hannah and I had been living together for a few years. Hannah had helped me to construct the Rainbow Fish Halloween costume I'd worn to the party. (We'd hot-glued broken CDs all over a felt fish suit so that it looked like it was covered in metallic scales. I took this costume off sometime between vodka number four and breaking a lawn chair in the backyard.) I looked forward to our family dinners every week, when we would sit around complicated salads and hold hands before dinner without irony. When Derek and Hannah got to the party, they lifted me into the front seat of Derek's Subaru, stopped frequently so I could throw up on the side of the street, and then climbed into my bed with me once we were home. I fell asleep sandwiched between two people who took turns rubbing my shoulders and cooing into my ears.

And in the back of my mind, I knew that it was okay, because I lived with people who loved me, and I loved them back. But it was also difficult to understand that it was okay right then. I had been so *sure* about Sam. We never really fought; we had terrific sex. I loved his mom and she loved me; she sent me once as a birthday present a meticulously homemade miniature mouse dressed to look like me. Sam and I could talk for hours and never run out of things to say. Sam loved to draw, and I loved his drawings. We had similar aesthetic sensibilities. We were both vegan, and neither of us drank. Everything *worked.* My bedroom wall was covered in Sam's art. His letters were littered around my room, because I liked finding them unexpectedly while looking for a T-shirt. I liked being reminded that I had all that *really* mattered in my life: true love.

The letters I'd hidden in my sock drawer and wedged between volumes on my bookshelf became the literal pieces of a broken relationship that needed to be picked up and dealt with. De-Samming my bedroom was emotional and painful. I cried all the time and didn't want to see anyone at all. I dressed in sweatpants and abstained from eye makeup. I listened to Alanis Morissette. When I wasn't rewatching *Gilmore Girls* for the nine-trillionth time, I wrote messy breakup songs and put them on the Internet, hoping Sam would find them. I wrote some pretty damning lyrics, let me tell you. Here's a taste: "All I want to do / is hate you. / It would probably be good for my health / to tell you to go fuck yourself."

This went on for months and months, and ultimately I decided that I was never going to go through a breakup like this one ever again. And so, naturally, I would need to never again be in a relationship like that. But at some point, once I'd started wearing jeans and eyeliner again, I felt like I badly needed to get laid. So I decided to try online dating.

Actually, at that point, online dating wasn't *entirely* new to me. When I'd first moved to New Orleans, I decided to post an ad on Craigslist—even though I was technically still dating Sean. I wanted to make friends in my new city; I figured my new BFF might very well be out there in the Internet's classifieds section. I posted my ad in the Platonic Only section, but Craigslist still makes you say you're either a W4M or a W4W (there was no W4Either One). I justified my posting in the W4M section by telling myself that I technically already had a number of female friends, if you counted my roommates (whom I had barely met and who I knew actively disliked me based on the number of times they said "I was just leaving" when I came into the kitchen). The truth was that I wanted someone to fall in love with me. Because of Sean, it felt wrong to fall in love with someone *myself*, but hey, what was the harm in getting a little attention from a good-looking single man? It didn't feel like cheating if I was only looking for some harmless attention.

I spent an hour crafting the kind of ad that I knew would bring an onslaught of horny boys. I titled my post "Seeking Partner in Crime. Must Love Pie." Here it is in its entirety:

I'm really, really lonely. I also suck at meeting people because I think I come on a little strong. I'm seeking a partner in crime. Past crimes have included: planting flowers where they don't belong (not a euphemism), making baked goods in dirty shapes, writing letters to strangers, sidewalk chalk murals. I understand that it may seem like I'm not a very dangerous criminal. I'm not. I like: Nintendo over PS, the Hornets (I have hella tickets for this season), *Scott Pilgrim* and kin, things related to birds, eating out, Charlie Parker, pie, catching lizards and/ or frogs. I dislike: sloppy drunks (I kind of am one, though, so I'm a hypocrite), super-lowbrow humor, crime drama shows, plain Hershey's chocolate, people who chew too loudly. Note the pie. I really like pie, and I like to make it for my friends. Lately I have had very few friends because I just (read: five months ago) moved here from Portland, Oregon, and things swing differently down south. But maybe you'll be one?

Because it's the future, I now have the rare opportunity to go back through this post, editing for full disclosure.

> I'm really, really lonely.
> *This wasn't untrue, but it wasn't really true, either. I was afraid my on-again-off-again boyfriend was going to go off-again. I hoped for innocent male attention just in case.*
> I also suck at meeting people because I think I come on a little strong.
> *I suck at meeting people because I don't actively try to do it very much. I also come on a little strong. That part is true.*
> I'm seeking a partner in crime.
> *Boys love that kind of thing.*
> Past crimes have included: planting flowers where they don't belong (not a euphemism),
> *I've never done this, but I've always wanted to. Once in high school I went as far as buying a potted zinnia and leaving it near a park. Looking back, I'm not sure what I meant, exactly, by "not a euphemism." Obviously, this was supposed to be sexual, but I don't know what "planting flowers where they don't belong" would mean in the sex world.*

making baked goods in dirty shapes,

This isn't true either, unless you count Santa cookies. Some people have kinks like that, I guess.

mailing letters to strangers,

How would a person even do this? With a phone book? Who had a phone book in 2008?

sidewalk chalk murals.

I did that once, but I was seven.

I understand that it may seem like I'm not a very dangerous criminal. I'm not. I like: Nintendo over PS,

I have no interest in video games at all. I mean, I'll casually come in thirteenth in Mario Kart over the holidays with my sister, but that is it. I had no idea that people shortened PlayStation to PS—I think I just assumed that that must be the case. I have literally zero preference on the subject of gaming platforms. It's amazing to me that I can even use the words "gaming platform" correctly.

the Hornets (I have hella tickets for this season),

The Hornets were the New Orleans basketball team at the time. The name has since switched to the (menacing-sounding) Pelicans. I like basketball okay, but it certainly wouldn't rank on a top-one-thousand list of my favorite things. I did not have "hella tickets" for that season, but I knew one could easily buy them on Craigslist. I clearly had a good working knowledge of Craigslist.

Scott Pilgrim and kin,

Scott Pilgrim is an indie comic-book legend, and I do really like the books. The movie hadn't come out yet, so this was still a cool thing to write. It was maybe a little too cool, because I didn't get a single response that referenced this talking point.

things related to birds,

True.

eating out,

False—I like to cook. I especially hate eating out in New Orleans because I'm a vegan, and when you say that at a restaurant there, the waiters think you mean that you want the seafood platter.

Charlie Parker,

This was a time when I thought hot girls listened to bebop-era jazz music exclusively. I don't remember why I thought this.

pie,

True.

catching lizards and/or frogs.

What?! No! I have never done this and will never do it. Leave lizards and frogs alone! I think I was trying to get across that I was boy-like in that I could abuse animals. But I'm not, and I can't.

I dislike: sloppy drunks (I kind of am one, though, so I'm a hypocrite),

See, gentlemen? I can be cool and easy-to-sleep-with if you need me to be.

super-lowbrow humor, crime drama shows, plain Hershey's chocolate, people who chew too loudly.

All of these are true.

Note the pie. I really like pie, and I like to make it for my friends. Lately I have had very few friends because I just (read: five months ago) moved here from Portland, Oregon,

Actually it was Walla Walla, Washington.

and things swing differently down south.

I thought this was a fun and quirky thing to say.

But maybe you'll be one?

Please answer.

Do you know who wrote back to that Craigslist post? *Hundreds of totally creepy, weird dudes.* What made them creepy and weird, you ask? Seventy-five percent of them attached pictures of their penises to the first email they sent me, and the other 25 percent offered. Well, no, that's not true; one guy was married and said that he and his wife were into bird-watching, but that they were also potentially looking for a third.

I didn't write back to—let alone meet in person—anyone who responded to my Craigslist ad. After about a month I stopped getting responses to it, and I decided I was done with online dating forever.

A few years later, when I *actually* decided to start dating around, I did attempt to do it in the old-fashioned, non-computer way. I figured out a trick to lure single people into bed with me, and I felt that it was basically foolproof: aggressive eye contact. I called it "aggressive eye contact," but really it was more like *insistent* eye contact, or *persistent* eye contact. Here's how it worked:

You found a person you wanted to kiss on the lips. You stared at them for as long as it took for them to notice. Then you locked eyes with them and tried to convey a look that was simultaneously shy, awestruck, and a little horny. That sounds complicated, but for me it was just a wide-eyed stare that I held for a full beat before lowering my forehead a little and doing an Audrey Hepburn–style half smile. That this blunt mating tactic worked so well for me is no coincidence: data from experiments that have been conducted since the 1970s backs up the notion that women who make the first move in a romantic encounter are usually rewarded for it, even if they're proverbially batting out of their league.

Women have trouble asking for what they want. That idea is the hallmark of Sheryl Sandberg's provocative *Lean In: Women, Work, and the Will to Lead*, and she made millions of dollars from it. In 2013 (when *Lean In* came out), the notion that women don't ask for what they want merited feature-length stories in *Forbes* and *Fast Company* and on NPR. The stories are always in partial listicle format; they lead with some kind of sociological study that suggests women are socialized to be "nice" and to not "ask," and follow with a sea of bullet-pointed advice: "Get good counsel," "Know your bottom line," "Do your homework," etc.

I don't love the *Lean In* mentality because it suggests that in order to make the business world better, women have to adjust to a culture that has been created by men. They must adapt to a male-dominated structure in order to get what they want. In dating, however, I wish women would ask for what they wanted. In the world of love and sex, asking for what you want—not demanding but *asking*—is not a game; it's the definition of communication.

Granted, all this speculation is *very* heteronormative. Women flirting with other women likely have different success rates (oh-so-shockingly, there's basically no long-term research on this subject), as must men flirting with men. And also, "batting out of their league"? Come on, researchers. That's not a real thing.

But for our purposes, let me just say that in my single life, I did very well with prolonged, engaged, and complex eye contact. I did so well with it, actually, that it had a 100 percent make-out session success rate.

I bragged about this while visiting my uncles in San Francisco over the summer. They told me I would have to prove myself, because they found my claim hard to believe. I said I would do it at the upscale vegan restaurant we were going to for dinner. (People who frequent upscale vegan restaurants are worth kissing: they usually have very shiny hair, possess an uncommonly self-actualized—if somewhat arrogant—moral compass, and never get sick.) At dinner, my uncles and I collaboratively picked out a guy with a (shiny) bun whose job it was to bring out the drinks and the salads. When he brought the salad to our table, I leaned forward and fixated on the side of his head until he noticed, and then let the eye contact begin. It was really good eye contact. It seemed to last for an hour. Eventually he shook his head as if he'd just woken up from a dream (such a good sign), and retreated to the restaurant's kitchen. This was going to be a success.

I would just have to wait until he came out again in order to try some flirtatious conversation. (In truth, the eye contact move is a one-two punch: you get the eye contact, and then, later, you make a kind of snarky comment. It's helpful if the comment is something that proves you're funny, cool, and dryly referential, such as: *I like the music they're playing here, but it makes me want to call myself in 1993 to tell past me to save my drop-crotch culottes; I had no idea the sounds of MC Hammer*

would be reincarnated so far into the future. You're welcome to use that if you want.) But the salad guy never came out again! We even ordered dessert, thinking the salad guy might also be the dessert guy, but he wasn't. I was very disappointed to have to head back to my uncles' house rather than to the apartment of a bun-wearing salad server.

I was not about to have my record tarnished; and so I launched my second-ever online dating attempt. I went on Craigslist again and posted a Missed Connection titled "Your Hair Was in a Bun," and listed the location as the name of the restaurant. The message itself was short:

> I was sitting with my uncles. You brought out the salads. We made eye contact, right?

No one ever responds to Missed Connections, but I'd never posted one, and it felt like a rite of passage I'd so far missed out on. There used to be a dozen or so listed in the back of the alternative weekly newspaper I read in high school, and I cut out the good ones to keep in a box as inspiration. (I don't know what I was trying to be inspired to do. I've always had a habit of collecting things "for inspiration" that end up in dusty piles in a basement or an attic.) The bun guy offered an opportunity, so I wrote my Missed Connection and then flew back to New Orleans and forgot about it. But a week later, as I sat in a professional development session on how to teach children to read the short *e* sound (apparently, it's not as obvious as the other vowels), I received this email:

> My coworkers brought this to my attention. It brought mirth to the eventless duration of our services this evening and flattered me quite.
>
> You were sitting in a booth near the host stand, right? If you're who I think you are, then it's a funny coincidence: I forgot until now, but that evening I almost considered mentioning to a certain one of the uncles sitting closest to the aisle that his sincerity was remarkable. Some people try to thank one for bringing salads and things but can't manage it without affectation. He had simplicity.

But enough about your uncle. (Are we the people we think we are?) I would be delighted to meet you sometime. I've acquired the happy habit of stopping in to hear jazz at a place near my apartment, Club Deluxe. We could meet there an evening soon; or somewhere else—wherever.

I know, right? This was straight-up Hollywood romance material. Premise: Missed Connection is connected via the Internet. Conflict: But the girl got on a plane and flew across the country! How will these two lost souls find each other? Hijinks, maybe? A scene with a dog? Anything's possible in the world of major motion pictures starring people like Meg Ryan.

I replied immediately that while jazz sounded great, I had only been visiting and was now back in New Orleans. But did this guy want to be my pen pal? He said yes, that sounded great. I got a postcard a week later; I sent off a package in return (I'm an overcompensator when it comes to mail); and we were off.

Craigslist waiter and I corresponded for a year, and finally I decided that we should rendezvous in person. I bought a plane ticket to San Francisco and met him at midnight at a downtown BART station. He was beautiful, but not as great as I had remembered. His hair was still in a bun (male buns were all the rage in my circle of friends, so this was a plus), but I could see now how he was balding a little in the front. He had one of those hunky cleft chins that are good in theory but which over time can start to remind you a little of Gaston from *Beauty and the Beast*. He was also not as tall as I was. Otherwise, though, he was dreamy, and he was reading something distinctly masculine: Thomas Pynchon or David Foster Wallace or Jack Kerouac or something.

After confirming that yes, we were the people we thought we were, we walked to his car and he drove me to his house. That's not quite right, actually; he didn't live in a house, or even an apartment. Craigslist guy lived on a boat in the Berkeley marina. You'd think that in a year of handwritten correspondence this boat-living thing would have come up, but it hadn't. I'd always sent my letters to a PO box and never questioned it.

On the boat, the Craigslist guy talked about how depressed he was, how meaningless life was, and how much he missed his ex-girlfriend. He played me songs about his ex-girlfriend on his acoustic guitar. I told him sad stories about teaching in New Orleans that I thought would impress him. He didn't seem all that interested in them. He wanted to know if I wanted to know how he had met his ex-girlfriend. I didn't, but he told me anyway. He'd seen her on a bench and simply had to sit down next to her and tell her how beautiful she was, and then they fell in love.

We slept in the tiny triangular cabin with a hospital cot–sized mattress inside. I made out with Craigslist guy, and he was a wet, clam-tongued kisser. Later, I went down on him, still holding out hope that our romantic comedy potential was greater than the so-far misfire that was our rendezvous. After I was done, he said, "Whoa. I didn't think that was going to happen." And then he fell asleep.

The next morning, he let me buy him breakfast, and after that I never saw him again.

When I got back to New Orleans, I decided to give online dating a try in earnest. OkCupid was more of a thing at that point, although none of my friends used it. I did know that, of the online dating sites, OkCupid was "the free one," so I signed up for an account. I set up a profile that was very specific—maybe obsessively so—about how I wasn't looking for anything serious right now and just kind of wanted to hook up with people in a fun and respectful way, and how, no, really, I wasn't kidding, I really was *not* looking for something serious right now. This was an attractive quality to a lot of men who were very unattractive to me. I got a lot of messages from guys who opened with "Hey, Little Tits, I'll fuck your brains out tonight if you want." (Or some iteration of that. Men online loved to tell me how small my breasts were and how they would still, heroically, have sex with me.)

I sent messages to two men and two women. The men were both musicians and played multiple instruments (one played jazz, the other mostly punk). I had never dated a musician before because I had read in plenty of books and magazines that it was bad news to date musicians. But I got on OkCupid because I was finally looking for a bad-news kind of person—insofar as "bad news" meant someone who didn't want to settle down. Plus, I was, like, a 96 percent match with both of those guys, and this was an era in my life when I naïvely trusted the Internet to provide conclusive algorithms concerning dating potential. The women were more interesting than the men (one was a burlesque dancer with a penchant for adopting rescue cats; the other was a former biology major who studied moss and loved *The Wonder Years*), but neither of them messaged me back. I could comfort myself with statistics on that one: OkCupid says that while 30 percent of straight men respond to initial messages they receive from women, only 25 percent of queer women do.[1]

The punk musician was out of town for a while, but he promised to get in touch with me when he got back. The jazz musician had stated in his profile that he was in a polyamorous partnership with a gender-neutral person. This was one of the first times I had seen someone use the word "polyamorous" in a real-life context, and it was very interesting to me. I wanted to know how that worked, and if he ever got jealous, and if he felt happy in his relationship or if it was lacking, and if he was dating anyone else. He patiently answered my questions via OkCupid messenger: it worked great; he got jealous sometimes; he loved his relationship; and he wasn't dating anyone else, but his partner was.

We both danced around the idea of maybe meeting up sometime, but neither of us had ever used the Internet to date before, and we both had trepidations. Rather than make a date, we engaged in an ever-swelling email correspondence. He told me that he lived in Mid-City, he was allergic to cats, and he was somewhat desperately applying for day jobs; I told him that I taught at an elementary school in Mid-City, I had two cats (named for jazz musicians), and I played the piano. (I acted like I played it well. That's what you do when you're trying to seduce a musician.)

My job at the time had me out of bed at 4:00 a.m., out the door by 6:30, home around 6:00 p.m., and preferably asleep by 8:00. This was not the schedule of a casual dater. Deep into our increasingly platonic email correspondence, I resigned myself to never meeting the jazz musician in actual life. During recess at school I sometimes daydreamed about going over to his hypothetical house that was, in my mind, teeming with brass instruments piled on top of each other. I imagined him making me sweet tea and then picking any old saxophone up off the floor to serenade me with something slow and sexy like "Satin Doll"—a sultry-sounding title for a song I had never heard played but had seen listed in books of jazz standards. This fantasy, I assumed, would begin and end my romantic relationship with the jazz musician.

But then during one Morning Meeting (an ugly ritual wherein all the teachers at school stood in a circle and did team-building chants), the vice principal announced that our school was pairing with a local arts organization, and a visiting artist—a musician—would work with a few teachers for a month to design a unit plan that integrated reading and music. That kind of thing was right up my alley, so I was the first to sign up to work with the musician. By now you've correctly guessed what I *never* would have guessed in a million years, because life is not usually *You've Got Mail*: of all the musicians in the city, our school had partnered with my OkCupid suitor.

Because we had never seen each other in person, and profile pictures can be deceiving (also, OkCupid has its participants go by only first names and southern elementary schools require only last ones from their teachers), it took a comically long time for us to realize what had happened. We sat down together in a tiny room with buzzing fluorescent lights to go over the teachers' edition of the reading manual. Then we started to piece things together:

We laughed about it, traded quips about fate, and made a date to get a drink on Friday to celebrate Sidney Bechet's birthday.

The date went great; we hit it off beautifully and made out on my front porch after he rode his bike all the way back to my house with me. The next weekend I met a cute special-education teacher from another school at a housewarming party. He talked at length about Weird Al Yankovic's movie, *UHF*. I took him home to fool around. That was also great. And then the OkCupid punk musician came back into town, and we went on a date to see a campy horror movie at an old puppet theater. We had a great make-out in the middle of a bright-lit street before parting ways to head home in opposite directions. I have to tell you: I was pretty proud of myself. I was having a lot of emotionless, super-great make-outs with three separate dudes, and none of us were getting into "relationships" with each other. I was hooking up! I was in the culture! I was loving it!

Except I wasn't just having great make-outs with these guys; I was accidentally really enjoying their company. The jazz musician parted ways with his partner a few days after we met, and he was devastated. After that, we spent most of our time together talking about heart-break and listening to moody jazz records with our eyes closed. The special-education teacher was one of the funniest, weirdest people I had ever met, and we decided to join a Dungeons & Dragons campaign together. And the punk guy showed up at my house one day wearing a suit and holding a box of Popsicles to share with me on a bridge. Very quickly, my careless hookups became meaningful relationships I felt invested in. Eventually I stopped physically hooking up with those guys, but I remained close friends with all of them. This infuriated me. I didn't think I needed more friends; I needed more *sex*!

Regardless of my fury, I failed to recognize my own patterns (sending follow-up text messages; choosing meaningful dates like going to amusement parks or for long rural bike rides; learning the names of all my hookups' friends and family members), and so I was doomed to repeat them. After things fizzled romantically with the jazz musician, the special educator, and the punk guy, I started afresh with a vegan baker, a teacher who worked in the school garden, and a former contestant on *The Biggest Loser*. We had some good hookups, and then I got to know these people, too, and eventually the friendship was better than the sex and everything fizzled all over again.

The paradoxical trouble was this: a hookup with someone you don't really know or like that much is not, at least in my experience, terribly fulfilling. This was proved by three separate one-night stands I had with people I met while traveling across the country on a comedy tour. Two of these were with women I hooked up with at bars. The most interesting affair, though, was with a man I saw at a taco stand and followed home. (He invited me; I didn't stalk him or anything.) He had *six pianos*. The sex lasted nine very boring minutes. Not knowing someone makes it difficult to articulate exactly how you want to hook up. You don't trust the person, and you don't think they trust you. It's sort of exciting to see a stranger's genitals, but after the novelty fades, there's not much pleasure to be had.

On the other hand, hooking up with someone you genuinely like, with whom you have shared weird jokes and sidelong public glances, is often *very* fulfilling. Holding out for a few dates before going all the way (whatever that may mean for you) is not necessarily conservative; it can be really hot. There's so much to explore on the human body, and a lot of incredible pleasure to be had without any body part physically entering any other body part. Herein lay my conundrum: meaningless sex yielded very little pleasure, but meaningful sex yielded the kinds of substantial relationships I thought I wanted to avoid.

I wanted to avoid them for all the same reasons that anyone who has just been dumped avoids them: the idea of getting hurt again is both terrifying and exhausting. Unfortunately, for many of us, there isn't a proverbial wall we can construct to keep intimate emotions out. But I wanted to have orgasms, and one-night stands weren't getting me there. I'm not saying they can't work for *anyone*, but I do think there are other people like me who need time and practice with a partner to have truly incredible sex. So what was I supposed to do? Should I sacrifice my heart in exchange for good sex, or abandon all hope of orgasm to maintain emotional apathy?

It struck me that maybe the trouble with love was not that it was inherently heartbreaking but that we see it inside a strict binary: either you're in love or you aren't. What if love was on more of a sliding scale?

For example, when Ben and I broke up, I didn't feel like I loved him any less, but I also no longer felt the kind of chemistry that made me want to have sex with him. Somehow I found a way to communicate that and Ben found a way to believe it, and we've been able to hold the word "love" between us for more than a decade. On the other hand, when Sam broke up with me, he told me he didn't love me anymore. Years later, I wonder if that was really true. Was it that he didn't love me anymore, or that he needed our relationship to change and he couldn't see any way down that didn't involve jumping off a cliff?

Of course, this idea isn't revolutionary, and it's far too broad to be universal. The "casual" relationship I had with the garden teacher is a good example. We dated for almost six months. We would spend the night together and then walk to the bayou and sit on cement blocks and eat baguettes with garlic hummus and cups of fruit and talk about everything from education justice to Dave Matthews Band. (He was pro DMB, I was anti, and yet we still had good make-outs.) I loved the garden teacher but was wary of being *in* love with him. I worried that being *in* love required the kind of monogamy I wasn't ready for. One day, we took a walk to see the irises bloom in the sculpture garden by the museum. We took turns naming the different varieties and sat on a bench under a shady tree to talk about our families. The weather was cinematic, and the garden was just empty enough to be peaceful. After the walk, he told me he was *in* love with me. I hugged him and kissed him like the character in the movie who's scared of love. After the L-word had been dropped, I freaked out. We kept taking long walks, but our conversations started to focus squarely on the nature of our relationship.

Again: I loved the garden teacher. I loved spending time with him, and I loved hooking up with him. But I started to worry that he wanted to hold hands in public. I got paranoid when I went out on dates with other people because it seemed like I might end up hurting him. The more I worried, the more I distanced myself; the more I distanced myself, the more I worried the distance would be hurtful. I didn't want to break up with the garden teacher, because my reason would be that I thought I was going to hurt him, and that's not a good reason to stop seeing someone—it sounds like a cop-out. But I felt that he should break up with me because he wanted a monogamous, in-love kind of relationship, something I couldn't give him.

Relationships get messy when two people want different things. A dangerous power dynamic can emerge if one person is more invested than the other, and ultimately, someone—or, more likely, both people—get wounded in the fray. This is definitely a flaw in my love-on-a-continuum relationship model. On the other hand, it's a flaw in *any* relationship model.

The other major flaw, of course, is time-related. I was never able to balance more than three romantic relationships at a time, and to be honest, maintaining even the three felt like I was pushing myself a little too hard. To get to know the jazz musician, the punk musician, and the special-education teacher intimately, I had to spend hours with them independently. If all I did in my life was date musicians and teachers, this would be almost manageable. However, I (like many people) had a full-time job and a separate catalog of platonic friends I wanted to prioritize. I had cats to play with and a mom to call at least once a week and chores to do. There weren't enough hours in the day, and frequently time management was the underlying cause of a romantic relationship fizzling into a casual friendship.

This period of casual dating, though, acted as the set of training wheels I needed to learn to ride the polyamory bicycle. While I dated around, I didn't use the word "polyamorous," but as I started to hear my friends use it more and more, I kept it in my lexicon as a tool I might use if I ever found myself accidentally falling head-over-heels in love again. Let me clarify: head-over-heels in love, *and* wanting to have sex. We really can't talk about polyamory without talking about sex, can we?

PART 4

Let's Talk about Sex

To some, polyamory seems to be *entirely* about sex. You might blame (or credit) *The Ethical Slut* for that. Dossie Easton and Janet W. Hardy's book (in its second edition) became a sort of Bible for the new polyamorists I hung out with in New Orleans. It's a great book. Per the authors' definition: "a slut is a person of any gender who celebrates sexuality according to the radical proposition that sex is nice and pleasure is good for you."[1] *The Ethical Slut* is written in the style of a guidebook—it's meant to delve into everything you need to know when navigating the brave new world of open relationships. But this is a book that is, at its heart, almost entirely about sex. It's about sexual adventure and the battling of sex negativity, which are important things. Polyamory isn't necessarily all about sex—but there's certainly a sexual element that should be discussed. Even if a polyamorous relationship is made up solely of asexual people, the *absence* of sex should be discussed.

Don't get me wrong: I loved *The Ethical Slut*. It fundamentally changed my life. One of the things that moved me so much when I read it was that it was written by women. I was woefully unused to seeing women write about, discuss, or even talk in passing about sex. I read *The Ethical Slut* almost ten years ago, and at that time, women writing about sex was a refreshing novelty. But now the happiness and intrigue has worn off, and I feel something else entirely: I'm angry.

That girls are taught not to talk about sex bothers me. It's more than that: girls are taught not to *enjoy* sex. We learn sex as a task or a job. When Peggy Orenstein wrote *Girls & Sex*, she wanted to know what sex was like for girls today; what she found disturbed her: "Even in consensual encounters, much of what the girls described was painful to hear."[2] To learn a little more about her research, see the box below. Personally, I remember the first time I checked out my vagina with a hand mirror. I was seven, and I thought my vagina was totally amazing. It looked like soft, lovely fabric; I was so glad I didn't have a horrible penis, which I knew was a fleshy extension that boys had to carry around. It wasn't until fifth grade that I learned everyone else thought vaginas were inferior to penises. Kent Jackson said he heard they were like dead fish. It seems most girls truly believe that everyone thinks vaginas are gross—especially their boyfriends.

More Horrifying Facts about Young Women and Sex

- The vast majority of the girls Orenstein interviewed did not have orgasms during intimate encounters.
- Women overwhelmingly think of fellatio as a "skill to master" and almost never as something reciprocal.
- Girls told interviewers that they didn't want to "subject" boys to their vaginas.
- Girls don't learn where their clitorises are (or, in many cases, that they even exist).

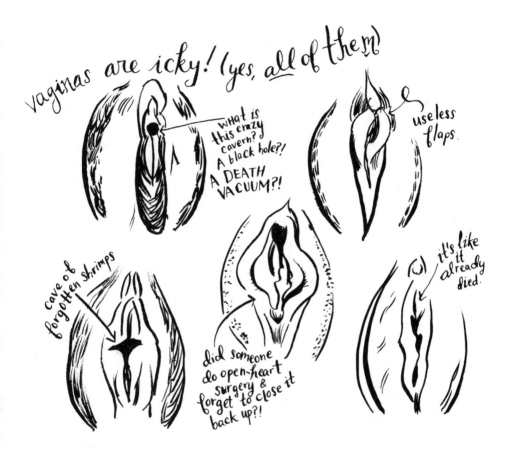

Pleasure, as a general rule, is not something people who are growing up are supposed to know much about. Girls and boys would be equally disadvantaged here if it weren't for the exponentially growing porn industry. Porn poses a deep quandary for me. First, I really enjoy watching porn, and (as I watch it on a near-daily basis) I'm glad it's readily available to me anywhere there's an Internet connection. On the other hand, pretty much every hormonal kid in the country learns what sex is supposed to look like (and more than that, what pleasure is supposed to look like) from watching porn; and porn is as comparable to actual sex as The Venetian casino in Las Vegas is to Venice, Italy. This is especially true for women and girls.

When I was in the seventh grade and the Internet was shiny and new, someone sent a spam email to my first email address titled, "You Have to C This." I had no knowledge of spam, or of how strangers could potentially access your email address to send you nasty computer viruses and suck money out of your bank account, or take your identity and live out a version of your life thousands of miles away from your physical being. I opened "You Have to C This" and found that it contained an attachment of a photograph, which loaded more slowly than today's youth could possibly conceptualize. The photograph materialized in horizontal strips: the first minute you got the top of a girl's head; five minutes later you could see to her neck; five minutes after that it became clear that she was wearing a schoolgirl's uniform. It took a full fifteen minutes before I finally saw what I was supposed to "C": the girl had lifted up her plaid skirt, and she was not wearing underpants. There was a thin strip of brown hair down the middle of her nether regions, in the shape of a piece of chewing gum.

I thought the picture of the partially nude schoolgirl was, to put it simply, wonderful. I printed it out on my parents' printer and stored it in an empty Valentine's Day chocolate box. It didn't take long for me to learn that you could search the Internet for all kinds of naughty pictures and stories; the schoolgirl picture was soon joined by a sixty-four-page piece of—surprise, surprise—literary erotica about *Boy Meets World*. The story had to do with Topanga's being salaciously curious to the point of having sex with every other character on the show—Corey's mom and Mr. Feeney included. I loved it so much that I felt disturbed by myself; it was as though I'd found out I had committed a grisly murder in my sleep; no one suspected me, but how could I live with myself?

But honestly, I'd known that I had an apparently unnatural interest in sexuality before the pornographic email. When I was four years old, I pressed my palms up between my legs and rocked back and forth, fantasizing about getting spanked on the bottom by a man with a mustache. I didn't think it was wrong until my mother told me it was—but looking back, I think she probably grappled with how to deal with this whole child-masturbation thing with a substantial amount of care. I get the sense that my mother didn't masturbate a whole lot as a young woman, and she might not have known exactly what she was supposed to do. She told me later that she thought I was having "rocking-horse dreams," until she got wise and told me to never do, um, "whatever it was [I was] doing" in public.

When I developed a crush on a boy whose name I'll protect (let's call him Rory), my fantasies got significantly stranger, but at least I knew how to hide them. I was six. (That might sound like a very similar age to four, but when you're six, four is ages ago.) I imagined Rory and I had both gotten arrested for some reason (we were being wrongfully convicted, but no one would listen to us). We were thought to be very dangerous, so we were handcuffed (naked) to a brick wall in a dungeon and made to stand on wooden boxes. And there, side by side, sure we were going to die, we had sex. Because I was six, I didn't know what sex was. All I knew was that it had to do with bathing-suit parts.

I didn't imagine the sex because I *couldn't* imagine it; I just thought about standing next to naked Rory, sentenced to death in a dungeon. I liked thinking about it, and I liked rocking back and forth on my palms while thinking about it, and I knew that all of it was very, very bad.

I had orgasms. I didn't know they were called that; there just always came a time when I was done rocking back and forth. In that moment, which came in a sudden dizzy rush, I was immediately ashamed of myself. I couldn't *believe* I had just rocked back and forth on my palms and thought about dirty images. I never wanted to do it again; in fact, I almost always promised myself I wouldn't.

It took me until the age of twenty-two to understand that plenty of self-respecting girls masturbated. I was twenty-six before I realized that I knew how to orgasm. I read a lot of *Cosmopolitan* magazine, and it made such a big deal out of having an orgasm. (The most recent feature I could find in *Cosmo* about female orgasms quotes a woman as saying, "It was like a volcanic eruption . . . but down there"; another woman says, "It feels like melting and exploding at the same time."[3] That may be true for many women, but I was waiting for lava to come out of my vagina, and that never happened.) I assumed that I was not having "an orgasm" when I had sex because I was not having sex right. By the time I was in college, I had unlimited access to free porn videos (the Internet grew *fast*), and I watched them sometimes with a pencil and paper, trying to figure out how to have one of these coveted feminine explosions.

Then one afternoon, while I was masturbating to a fine selection of literary erotica (still my favorite format, even with said access to all the videos and high-definition photos I could ever want), I read the line, "I came to completion." It wasn't a very poetic (or even technically correct) sentence, but when I read the word "completion," something clicked for me. "Oh," I thought. "Maybe an orgasm is just when I feel like I'm satisfied. Maybe it's just when I'm done." To have an orgasm while I was having sex, I had to move slowly and push my body against my partner's body the way I pushed my palms against my body. It wasn't really that hard, actually; but it was very different from the way the girls in porn videos seemed to do it.

Considering how early to the masturbation game I had been, it's surprising that I discovered feminist sex so late in life. It came to me in slow stages. The first time I decided that I wanted to prioritize my own orgasm during sex with a man was with Sam. I was twenty-five years old, and I had never done that before. It felt like eating an entire birthday cake on someone else's birthday, but I went for it anyway. It wasn't until we had been dating for two years that I felt comfortable telling him I wanted to try to have an orgasm. He was into that idea, because he was not a monster. It took an hour. There was a part in the middle when I sat on the edge of my bed and cried because I didn't think I would be able to get there. But it was Saturday morning and we had nowhere to go, so we kept trying and kept trying until, finally, I went over the edge.

And it was fucking awesome.

That sentence—"And it was fucking awesome"—is its own paragraph because I cannot believe how long I waited to really enjoy having sex, and I'm sad about it. I'm sad that no one ever told me girls had just as much right to sexuality as boys. I wish someone had grabbed me by the shoulders and shaken me and told me sex could be amazing, but that the secret to it was not in porn or in books or in conversations with therapists. The secret to sex was to try as hard as you could to enjoy it. You should spend a lot of time with your own sex parts figuring out which buttons you like pushed and how you like them pushed. I saw sexy women having a very specific kind of sexy sex in movies and on HBO shows, but I never saw women bending awkwardly over their partners' bodies to get a certain angle or moving slowly in the dark with closed eyes. (No, not even on *Girls*.)

If I ever have a daughter and I could teach her one thing (besides "be kind" and "even if gluten allergies are real, bread is too good to not eat"), it would be this: You have just as much say over your sex life as your partner has. If you want to be done with sex, then sex is over. If you want to keep going, then you should be allowed to keep going. That the duration of a sexual experience is so often determined by the hardness of a penis is small-minded and, frankly, boring.

How long do you like to wait before having sex with someone?
What are your favorite positions?
What is your sexual health like? When was the last time you were tested?
What line should never be crossed for you?
Do you have any triggers I should know about?
Is there anything you're curious about trying?
When would you feel comfortable trying that thing you're curious about trying?
Can we establish a safe word, just in case?
If you come first, you'll be ok with it if I want to keep going, maybe with this little vibrating toy I have... right?
Is there any position or pose you dislike?

Now, if only having good sex forever and ever was that easy. My first orgasm didn't necessarily beget a whole bunch of other orgasms as I had more sex. I dated some men I found easy to talk to about sex, and with those men I had orgasms more often. I dated some men who had no interest in talking with me about sex, and they were the ones who went at the whole thing hard and fast, with gritted teeth and tensed muscles. (Sometimes, looking up at men who had sex with me like that, I found it very difficult not to laugh. They looked so silly and false, like boys pretending to be sheriffs.) I dated a few women who helped me better understand how to talk openly and honestly about sex. I was so lucky to meet women who had done this sexual legwork already; they probably didn't realize it, but they were modeling conversations I would practice for the rest of my life.

For example, on the previous page you'll find a list of questions you can ask before you have sex with someone if you want the sex to be good. (Keep in mind that you should answer these questions, too; sex is a two-way street.)

Importantly, sex is generally (but not always) what separates platonic relationships from romantic ones. And so it should go without saying that sexual compatibility is incredibly important when forming romantic bonds with someone. This is something Dan Savage talks about a lot in his column and on his podcast: while he concedes that "other shit matters, too, of course—stuff like emotional compatibility, similar life goals, being on the same page about kids, etc.," he emphasizes that basic sexual compatibility is essential. "Its absence will eventually undermine everything else."[4]

When we spoke on the phone, Savage told me that the same is basically true about ideas around relationship structures. "If one person feels like they can't be in a poly relationship and the other person feels like they have to be, then, well, I'd say that relationship is doomed," he told me. One of the most wonderful things about polyamory is that it allows you to acknowledge that you will have similarities and differences with the people in your life; maybe the person with whom you're most sexually compatible isn't the same person with whom you're most emotionally compatible, and that's okay—because you can prioritize *both* of those people in significant ways. If sex is a major part of your life (it's a major part of my life), it's worth knowing a little about what you want so that you can put it on the table when you start to enter into new partnerships.

It took me a while to figure all this out. The people I casually (and not-so-casually) dated bore the brunt of my sexual exploration, and they did it with aplomb. By the time I called myself a polyamorist, I knew that I liked a little more kink than most of the people I'd slept with did. I had my feelers out for someone who owned ropes and knew how to use them.

I met Bob at a summer arts camp where we both worked. I'd been seeing my partner Luke for almost a year at that point, and Bob was the first new person I was interested in since the beginning of my and Luke's time together. Integrating Bob into my love life wasn't easy; there were a lot of conversations and a lot of jealousy, but I'd like to fast-forward to the good part, just for the purposes of sexual exploration. I'll get back to the superfun jealousy stuff later, I promise.

Bob and I talked about sex as soon as we started kissing. We wrote long emails to each other about sex that were almost clinical at first, asking questions like a med-school student trying to impress a doctor. I went back through our email threads while writing this book and found so much that impresses me. At one point I wrote, "An erection is not necessary for a great time; I've come to be one of those people who thinks there's too much pressure on penetrative sex, and that it can be kind of a downer for both parties." Great point, Past Sophie! When we had sex for the first time, Bob knew more about what I liked than most of the people I'd dated long-term had. As a result, the sex was very good. It continued to be good. Actually, it only got better.

Luke and I communicated about sex, too—a lot. We also had tremendously good sex. But there were some fundamental sex-communication questions that Luke and Bob each answered differently. For example:

My own answers, if you haven't already guessed, more closely resembled Bob's. Before Luke and I had sex for the first time, I asked him what he liked. He told me he liked kissing and rolling around, mostly, but he was "open to other stuff." Bob, on the other hand, had written me a novel about the kinky, dominant sex acts he had responsibly explored before our own genitals even entered the equation. Having a sexual relationship with Bob allowed me to live out my sexual fantasies with someone I knew was just as into them as I was.

But let's go back to Luke's answers for a minute. There's really nothing better than being with someone whose biggest turn-on is your pleasure. It's a dream come true when you find someone who keeps condoms around all the time. It's amazing when your lover is willing to try whatever it is you're into. I'm still making up for a young adulthood full of sexual missteps and trauma with a current sex life that's characterized by constant communication and lots and lots of female orgasms. Yay.

And it's not really my fault that I was so misinformed about sex. When I was growing up, sex education—even in Oregon, where laws were more lax—was piecemeal at best. Since the dawn of humanity (I'm guessing), adults have grappled with how to talk to kids about sex. In the 1990s and early '00s, America underwent a fresh crisis on the subject.

A Brief History of Hooking Up in America

1920s: An increase in automobile use leads to an increase in young people dating.

1940: Emma Goldman, who proclaimed that "marriage and love have nothing in common," dies, sending notions of free love into relative obscurity for over a decade.

1960s: The sexual revolution famously terrifies conservative family types.

1961: Robert A. Heinlein publishes the science fiction novel *Stranger in a Strange Land*, about an alien so put off by sexual possessiveness that he starts his own religion.

1980s: The AIDS crisis transforms sex into an even greater media villain.

2002: Meg Meeker publishes *Epidemic: How Teen Sex Is Killing Our Kids*, which introduces the (frankly impossible) concept of the "rainbow party": a get-together where girls allegedly put on different colors of lipstick and then take turns giving the same guy a blow job so their lipstick line might indicate who could go the deepest.

2009: $50 million in federal funding goes toward abstinence-only sexual education programming.[5]

2017: Donald Trump proposes a budget that would devote $277 million to "extend[ing] abstinence education and personal responsibility education programs" between 2018 and 2024.

These days, schools that offer more extensive programming still almost unilaterally come at sex education from a risk-based point of view. The dominant message is: "If, for some inexplicable reason, like maybe your brain is temporarily taken over by aliens, or maybe you get momentarily bad and rebellious and start listening to the Misfits because all your friends are, you might, *maybe*, find yourself, terrifyingly, acquiescing to having sex with someone. *Let's hope this doesn't happen*, but in the worst-case scenario—because even airplanes have to have procedures for what you should do if they crash—you ought to know how to use this condom. Keep one condom tucked in a locked pocket of your purse at all times. You definitely won't need more than one, because if by some horrible circumstance you *do* have sex, *trust us*: you won't want to have it again."

But teens keep having sex (surprise, surprise), and college kids *especially* keep having sex, and the semi-recent rise of dating apps like OkCupid and Tinder have made hookups easier than ever to come by. There have been waves of opinions about this: *Vanity Fair* called this culture a "Dating Apocalypse,"[6] and just a few months later *Vogue* countered that it was "the biggest NBD ever."[7] There's been quite a back-and-forth to this effect: terrified parents trumpet the horrors of hookup culture; horny young people tell them to chill out; someone says that hookup culture promotes rape culture; someone else says that saying hookup culture promotes rape culture is antifeminist.

For me, being able to combine feminist sex on my own terms with meaningful emotional relationships was the witches' brew that brought me to polyamory. Yes, there was sex. Yes, there was love. Yes, there were more than two consenting adults. And yes, the transition into this kind of model led to the best relationships of my life.

PART 5

Many Love

In my early twenties, I watched long-term relationship after long-term relationship blossom and fall apart in my life. For a long time, I held on to my mom's ideal of finding "The One," but it seemed like every "One" consistently faded into "Just Another One." I began to wonder if this whole head-over-heels-in-love thing was really for me. In order to keep myself protected, I applied "science" to my dating life. I put "science" in quotes because I mean that I constructed a set of categories, with the input and advice of no one at all, that I felt definitely described all the different kinds of love.

If I could just avoid the two last and deepest types, I figured I would be safe.

I've always been attracted to the idea that love is ultimately about chemicals, survival, something intrinsic and biological and unavoidable. But, in fact, evolutionarily speaking, love is tricky. We can't identify another species that definitely experiences it, and it sure causes a lot of trouble without much obvious biological payoff.

To that effect, my categories served me well. They allowed me to sort through my feelings mathematically, by shape and color. Treating dangerous emotions like so many fishing lures wore the costume of control.

The Five Categories of Love:

ONE: You go on a date or two with a person. You like the person, & you kiss the person, but you AREN'T REALLY that into it, so when they ask you on a third date, you say your SISTER is in town, even if she isn't, & when you SEE THEM at a function later on, you say HI, & maybe HUG, BUT you DO NOT say you would like to hang out sometime.

TWO: You go on three to five dates with a person, & you DEFINITELY make out with them,

(& probably you do more than that), you invite the person to functions, but you DON'T hold hands, although you might share food OR EVEN sleep over.

THREE:
You date the person regularly, more than five times at least; the person is a FIXTURE in your life & your roommates assume that the person will likely eat breakfast at your house on Sunday mornings (because the person ALWAYS sleeps over Saturday.)

pizza for breakfast.

Sexy.

FOUR: You LOSE CONTROL over how you're feeling. This is what is meant when people say "In LOVE!" You would be HEARTBROKEN if the person was no longer in your life, & not because your ego would be hurt but because you feel something about this person that BORDERS ON what other people describe as ADDICTION.   YOU ARE AT RISK.

YOU WILL inevitably GET HURT.
You continue to date this person because it is all you want to do in the world.

(FIVE is the same as FOUR, except that it is completely & honestly reciprocal.)

see this gooey, faraway look?
BEWARE

CATEGORY FIVE LOVE IS APPARENTLY WHAT EVERYONE IS LOOKING FOR.

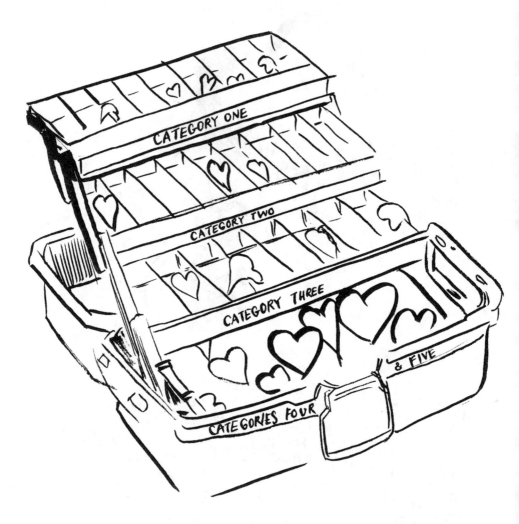

But my self-assuredness was interrupted in the midst of my dating-around phase when I met a tall, squinty-eyed gardener named Jesse. He cooked wonderful vegetarian shepherd's pie and actively listened more than he talked. He also knew a lot about insects, which was weirdly hot. I kissed him on the lips in my bedroom one night after dinner, and the next day he showed up on my doorstep to give me a letter that said, among other things, "I think love is just when you want someone else to be happy. So I'm going to write this:"

This sent my neat little tackle box into a full-on tailspin. I'd known Jesse for less than a week, and he was saying (or, rather, writing) "I love you." How unorthodox! Leave it to a handsome gardener to throw caution to the wind. I should have known. Had I learned nothing from romance novels?

That letter, though, was ultimately one of the greatest gifts I would ever receive—and not just because it came bundled with a burned

CD of delicate acoustic ballads by under-the-radar singer-songwriters. Although Jesse and I went on to have a somewhat fraught romance, that notion—that "love" could be simply "want[ing] someone else to be happy"—lingered. The letter popped into my head years later when I was reading an article in *Glamour* magazine about commitment. It was titled "Men and Commitment: By the Numbers," and was basically the results of a survey of a thousand men who gave their thoughts and feelings about "commitment," in this case meaning "long-term monogamy."

You've heard that before, right? "When is he going to commit?" "I'm committed, so what's holding him up?" "Now that you've locked him down with that ring, you know he's committed." But if I got to choose between being with someone who told me about the feelings he or she might be having for another person or being with someone who felt obligated to lie to me about those feelings, I would not only choose the former, I'd argue that the former was *more* committed.

The colloquial definitions of "love" and "commitment" have to be flexible in order to accommodate different types of relationships. It's not ultimately necessary that we all share the same definitions of these words; it's only necessary that we know what they can mean for ourselves, and that we constantly reevaluate what they mean. Humans change all the time; our definitions are allowed to change with us.

My definition of "commitment" was changing when I read that article in *Glamour*; at the time, I was in what I felt was the most committed relationship I'd ever had—and, incidentally, the first officially polyamorous one. After reading the article, I took to my blog and unloaded: "This relationship, for the first time in my life, is about taking care of myself and loving myself first and foremost; then trusting that [he] will do the same for himself; and then working together to build support and recognize not only each other, but the other people we are seeing. At the end of the day, being in my own 'monogamish' relationship feels like a pretty big commitment. It feels like I have a partner who is invested in his own happiness, just as he is invested in mine (and vice versa). That means being honest about what we want, and trusting each other to talk about it."[1]

The relationship was with a man named Jaedon. We met while I was substitute teaching at a New Orleans elementary school. We went on a few dates, and, although he was a full six years younger than me (and we were in our midtwenties, so that mattered), I fell in love with him.

I didn't mean to do that. I'd been battling this being-in-love-with-people thing for a long time and couldn't understand why it kept following me around. No matter how much I insisted that I "didn't want anything serious" or was "only interested in being a third," I kept finding myself falling in love—and more than that, finding that the love was reciprocated! Every time this happened, I freaked out. Post-Sam, if you recall, I'd decided that I was *not looking for love*. So when someone told me they loved me, I tended to distance myself, cry a lot, and ultimately say something like, "Sorry, but this isn't working for me." Or, worse, I would treat the person I loved like shit until *they* said "Sorry, but this isn't working for me." Why did I keep falling in love? I didn't know. I felt dysfunctional.

So when I fell in love with Jaedon, I hadn't meant to, but I also wasn't surprised. This time, though, I decided to try a new tactic: rather than running away from Jaedon, screaming, "I CAN'T DO THIS I AM A MONSTER I HATE LOVE NEVER TALK TO ME AGAIN" (or some version of that), I said to him, "What do you think about being in a polyamorous partnership?" He said he was into it, and that that was just what he wanted. This was going to be great! And so we decided to try.

We made rules. We didn't write them down, because they were simple: you had to tell the other person if you were going to go on a date; the other person had the right to veto; and if you were going to have a slutty one-time hookup, it was okay if you told the other person right afterward instead of right before.

There were typical, to-be-expected hiccups. I use the term "hiccups" here to mean "violent jealousy." I started dating other people first, and I chose someone Jaedon had gone to college with. When I called Jaedon to ask him if it would be okay for me to go out on a date with this guy,

I went on the date anyway, and we had a fun make-out. Afterward, Jaedon and I conversationally processed the whole ordeal for at least three hours. "Processing" is probably the most important word in most early polyamorous relationships. It's a euphemism that refers to what people do when they know they shouldn't be mad, but everything in their body is telling them to be mad. I would love to tell you that Jaedon and I got to a place where processing took less time, but we never did. On the other hand, I do think we processed things very civilly. We never yelled at each other, and we didn't interrupt each other, either. We listened, reflected, empathized, took long breaths, rescheduled appointments to "honor this conversation," and had reassuring after-processing sex over and over again. In fact, these conversations were at the center of why I felt that we were so committed to each other. They took a long time, and they were utterly respectful. As I listened to Jaedon and argued with Jaedon, I thought, "I have never loved someone as much as I do this person right now."

Our romantic relationship was wonderful, but it didn't last forever. One night a few months in, Jaedon and I were playing on Tinder side by side on a couch (what a fun couple we were!), and a guy appeared on my screen whom I had had a crush on for years. He was a guy I'd referred to for a long time as "*the guy*," in italics, because I didn't know his name. We were in tangential friend circles but had never met. He seemed like the kind of person who would have a girlfriend (read: he was SUPERhot), so I never mustered the courage to introduce myself to him. One time I saw him at the school where I taught (I later found out that he worked for an education nonprofit) and followed him around for a good fifteen minutes, trying to no avail to engage him in aggressive eye contact. He was my hunky, faraway New Orleans crush, and here he was on my Tinder screen, which implied that he did *not* have a girlfriend and that he would maybe *date me*.

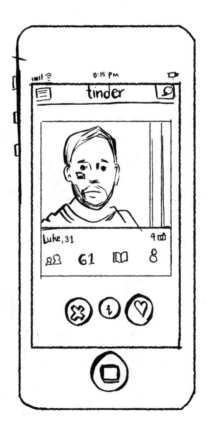

"Holy shit, Jaedon, it's *the guy*—the one I've been stalking for years!" I showed my phone to Jaedon so he could see *the guy* (Tinder informed me that his name was Luke).

"Oh, yeah," Jaedon said. "That's my boss." (*THAT WAS HIS BOSS!? WHAT?!* New Orleans is a *very* small city.) He paused. "You should swipe right." The tone of Jaedon's "You should swipe right" was not wholly convincing. While I could tell that he wouldn't have a problem with me swiping right, I could also tell that he wasn't thrilled that I'd referred to this guy as *the guy*. I couldn't blame him. Had the tables been turned—had Jaedon found a spectacular woman on Tinder whom he'd had a crush on for years and who was also my boss—I would have been nauseated. But, see, this was *the guy*. I swiped right.

This is the moment people who are trying out polyamory for the first time are simultaneously terrified of and excited about: the moment when someone in the relationship really falls for someone else for the first time. In theory, this moment is fine; in fact, it's terrific! This is the moment when you get to show how cool you are about everything; you get to demonstrate that, yeah, you can *totally* love two people at one time, or you can *absolutely* be happy for your partner to love two people at one time, or you are *utterly* excited about going on a three-way date with a person you and your partner just met at a party. In practice, at least for me and for the people I've loved, this moment is secretly stomach-turning and terrifying and exhilarating. Your body revolts against your mind; you want to feel chill and laid back, but instead you get a whole mess of emotions you didn't ask for.

With Jaedon and Luke, I was in the arguably easier position. I had the power because I was in control, I believed, of where my love went. I trusted myself to continue to be committed to Jaedon, and that was easy to do because I spend a lot of time in my own brain, monitoring my emotions. Jaedon was the one who had to wonder. If I stayed out an hour later than I had planned to, he had to wonder why. If I wanted to take Luke to a movie or a concert or a book reading, Jaedon had to wonder why I hadn't invited him. He had to trust me—a person he'd known for only a year—to keep my promises and keep him safe. I was holding him over a ledge, and he had to trust that I wasn't going to drop him.

After we matched, I sent Luke a message, my first ever on Tinder. It said:

> I have to tell you this because this is the perfect opportunity: I have had a crush on you for years. Once I followed you around Langston Hughes Academy.

He responded the next day:

> Oh cool! I think you are amazing! It's funny, I just did an interview with a journalist from NYC and we talked a lot about Tindering in a small community like New Orleans vs. a place like New York and how here you kind of have to be prepared to know or at least recognize most people.

Did you see that? He said he thought I was "amazing."

We chatted a little through the Tinder app, and I learned that Luke did not like fake mustaches or Bob Marley T-shirts, and that he was recently out of a relationship. He said he was "trying to figure out what kind of life he wanted to lead" and that his "love life was in limbo." I offered to buy him a drink, he said sure, and then that was the end of our correspondence for a few weeks.

Then my friend Molly—with whom I organized stand-up comedy shows—decided to throw a Molly-themed trivia night at a bar for her birthday. I liked this idea, because I hate regular birthday parties where you have to talk to people you don't know; a trivia night provided an activity that would effectively prevent any actual social interaction. I showed up at the bar without a team, hoping to scrape one together once I got there. I arrived early—earlier than Molly, even—and sat awkwardly in the wet corner by the out-of-order jukebox, hoping I wouldn't be noticed so I wouldn't have to order a drink.

After an interminable ten minutes, Molly came in with a suited-up guy on one arm and a tray of vanilla cupcakes in the other.

"Sophie! You're so . . . early and alone!" she said. Frankly, I was grateful that someone was talking to me. I was about to start making origami swans out of cocktail napkins.

"Yeah, I don't have a team," I said.

"Okay! That's okay! Darren doesn't, either!" She pushed the guy on her arm in my direction. "Darren! Sophie's going to be on your team! You guys are a team now! Oh, and also I think my roommate is coming, and he doesn't have a team. He's just bringing in the rest of the cupcakes."

And yes, Molly and Luke were roommates; and hey, guess what, he *also* didn't have a trivia team; and so I ended up on a trivia team with a man in a suit (whom I think Molly was probably sleeping with) named Darren and a man I had been infatuated with from afar for half a decade. A few minutes later, Luke's sister and her boyfriend showed up, and our team of mostly strangers swelled to a formidable five. We named our team Weezer, and won by a margin so large that the second-place team didn't have even half our point total.

There was a little bit of a spark between Luke and me, but it was nothing major. Sometimes (uh, usually) when you meet someone in real life, they're just not as good as your fantasy (I'm looking at you, Craigslist Boat Guy). He was fine, but I was very in love with Jaedon and didn't really see things going anywhere with Luke. I felt satisfied knowing that I'd met *the guy* in real life, and that he had been good at trivia, and that that had been that.

Luke, however, did not feel completely "that had been that" about *me*. He texted the next day to ask if I was going to a gala our mutual friends were throwing at the Pharmacy Museum. Since we ran in adjacent crowds (my stand-up partner was his roommate, for heaven's sake), we were often invited to the same events. I told him that, yeah, I was going, and he texted back, "Cool," and then I kind of forgot about the exchange; I was too invested in my relationship with Jaedon to be really thinking about anyone else—not even *the guy*.

The night of the function, I had a friend over for dinner, and we got into one of those conversations—this time it was about the emotional trauma of buying a house—that went on for a lot longer than anyone thought it would. By the time we'd wrapped up (way after we'd finished eating dinner and dessert, and had finished the bottle of wine, and had washed all the dishes), it was late. I asked my friend if she still wanted to go to this Pharmacy Museum party, and she said, "Why not?"

The Pharmacy Museum is filled with glass balls and tin cans of ointments. There are arm-length needles locked up in cabinets and blue bottles of "miracle tonic" on the shelves. There's a faintly antiseptic scent to the whole place that makes it feel like you're hanging out in a closed-down hospital. The space of the museum itself, however, is small—it's three stories tall, but each story consists of one room about the size of a modest living room. I'd been to the Pharmacy Museum only during the day; when I walked through it at night, my immediate thought was, "Why would someone want to throw a party here? It's barely a step up from being an actual haunted house."

But the museum had a courtyard, as do many of the buildings in the French Quarter. The courtyard was huge; hundreds of people schmoozed in summery semiformal outfits (per the invitation), holding plastic cups of white wine and throwing their heads back to laugh as though they were aristocrats in a period drama. I began to wonder how long I had to stay in order to honestly claim that I'd made an appearance. Five minutes? Seven?

Luke ambled up in the middle of this contemplation.

SOPHIE! I was beginning to think you WEREN'T gonna SHOW.

I liked that he was the only one at the gala who had completely ignored the wardrobe request.

Much later I would learn that Luke had thought that by asking me if I was going to this party, he was asking me on a date. When I showed up three hours late, he thought I was playing hard to get, but he still assumed that we were on a date. At no point during the evening, however, did I consider being at the Pharmacy Museum function with Luke a date. I was excited to see him, so I stood next to him while my friend went to use the restroom, but I didn't intend to stay there; the party was boring and I wanted to leave. Since the first time we met we'd been involved in trivia, I didn't know much about his life. I asked him to tell me a little about himself, and the first thing he said was that he was on the board of a charter school.

That, it turned out, was a bad place to start. I have a lot of very loud opinions about the charter school system in New Orleans. I can literally talk about it for hours without stopping to breathe. Since this is a book about love and not about charter schools, here's the short version: I hate the charter school system in New Orleans with the fire of a thousand political pundits. I spent an hour scolding Luke for being on the board of a charter school. I didn't let him get a word in edgewise. He could say nothing to assuage my doubts about him. He was not the man for me, and now I knew that for sure, and so after an hour on my soapbox, I stepped down and tried to find a friend at the party I could pawn Luke off on.

But Luke didn't want to be pawned off, and he followed me into every conversation I started with another person; he paid for my white wine when I went to the drinks table; he waited for me when I went to the bathroom. When I finally got myself together enough to leave the party, he walked me to the door and hugged me good-bye. "He's nice, but dumb," I thought. I went to Jaedon's house afterward and climbed into bed with him. "I saw Luke tonight. Turns out we have nothing in common. He totally sucks." I was satisfied with that reality and fell asleep easily despite the perpetual clicking of the ceiling fan.

The next day, however, Luke sent me another text message. It said, "Do you want to go on a date?"

Obviously, I didn't *really* want to go on a date with Luke. Had he texted, "Do you want to catch up over coffee sometime?" I'd have given him a firm no. But I had never actually been asked out on a date (when someone uses the word "date" in the asking) before. That's not how it happens in the modern world; you leave the door open when you invite someone to do something just in case they're not into it. You say, "Would you want to grab dinner sometime?" That way, if you get to dinner and the person you invited is aloof and detached, you can talk about *Game of Thrones* and salvage some of your dignity when you go home alone. Asking someone on an out-and-out date was a gutsy move. I admired Luke's directness, his honesty. And I was also flattered, because I'd spent the entirety of a party scolding this guy and trying to get away from him, and here he was, asking me on a date, so I must be something special, huh? Anyway, what was two hours on a Friday night? It was nothing, really. So I said yes.

I said yes, but I added the caveat you have to add when you're in a good, communicative, open relationship. My Tinder profile stipulated that I was "poly and partnered," but just to be totally transparent, I texted Luke back that I had a primary partner and we were open; I wanted to make sure that wasn't a deal-breaker. Luke texted back that he knew I was dating Jaedon (he had clearly done his Facebook home-work). He worked with Jaedon, remember? He liked him very much. He was cool with dating someone in an open relationship. And so the date got the green light.

We met at a bar where cigarette smoke clouded up the pool tables and people had to shout over the blasting wall television. The bar was crowded, and all the tables were occupied—some so much so that women were sitting on top of them. We decided to get a bottle of wine and some chocolate at the market nearby and sit on the bridge over the bayou instead.

Not to brag, but I'm good at first dates. I chalk this up to my incredible ability to ask fun and unique personal questions (and follow-up questions) in a way that implies that I'm genuinely interested in the answers. This ability comes from spending my formative years eating lunch alone in my English teacher's classroom, vowing that if I ever got to go on a date with a boy, I would make him feel like the most special person on earth. I kept a list of questions on a pale pink notepad, and added to it throughout middle school and into high school. I began to collect questions the way other people collect stamps or state quarters.

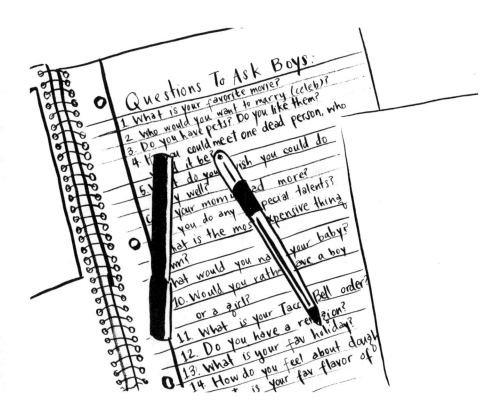

After Luke and I had picked out an Argentinian Malbec (Luke is from Argentina; I can't tell the difference between any wines—not even between whites and reds, or between wines that have gone bad and ones that cost a thousand dollars a bottle), we strolled along the old stone road lit up with Christmas lights strung on a wire running along the oak trees. I'd come up with my first question while we stood in the checkout line and opened my mouth to ask it: "What was the last album you really liked?" Only I didn't say it. Luke did.

Every time I tried to turn the conversation to him by asking a provocative question, Luke answered but then immediately asked me something in return. As we reached the bridge where we'd decided to sit, I was knee-deep in a story about the time my family went to the Bahamas when I was fourteen. This was perfectly strange; I wondered if I had met my match.

Luke asked me what animal I was at heart (I know—this date was interesting *and* whimsical!), and I told Luke that I thought I was a macaw. Macaws are vegetarians, they're big and loud, and, hauntingly, they self-mutilate when they feel distressed or lonely (by plucking out their feathers). This, incidentally, was the cutest way I'd ever found to tell a person that I struggle with self-mutilation. Luke perked up, telling me that he would be a bird, too.

I told Luke that I had a sparrow tattooed on the back of my neck. I used to think they mated for life, I said. He said, "Huh. I just like them because they're adventurous."

And then, of course, I fell in love with Luke. Not on that date, but a few dates later. The moment I knew I was going to fall in love with him was a Tuesday evening when Hannah and I were making salad for dinner (Hannah and Derek and I had, at this point, been living together for five years). Luke showed up unannounced and gave me a mixtape he'd made for me. Over dinner, Hannah and I put the tape on the stereo. It was very cool that Luke had made an actual tape in the first place. I mean, when was the last time someone gave you a physical cassette with a playlist on it? That's right—it was probably 1991. In 2014, a mixtape was a very kitschy, hipster-in-a-hot-way kind of move. On top of that, the guy was a master of mixtapes. Midway through its second loop, I walked over to the stereo and pushed the stop button. "Oh no, Hannah," I said. "This situation is going to hurt."

I couldn't see how I could possibly maintain a relationship with Jaedon and go through these falling-in-love motions with Luke at the same time. I didn't know how Jaedon was supposed to not feel jealous when I told him about this extraordinary mixtape. I didn't know how Luke was supposed to continue to want to make me mixtapes if I was always spending Valentine's Day with someone else. Everything felt, in the moment, too heightened to last. Later, I would learn that there are ways to make nearly any romantic situation—even impossible-seeming ones—work. In this case, though, I was right.

My priorities around Jaedon and Luke started to change. I began wanting to spend more time with Luke than Jaedon was comfortable with. There were only a few times that Jaedon and Luke and I all ended up at the same event—sometimes I did big comedy shows and invited them both, because you're supposed to hustle tickets when you're trying to make it in stand-up. I always decided beforehand which of them I was going to hang out with after the show; that decision was usually discussed with Jaedon first, and then communicated to Luke. I remember standing awkwardly between Jaedon and Luke outside an indie movie theater one time after a show, just before Luke and I were about to head out for dessert. Jaedon and Luke kept calling each other "man"—as in, "Hey, man, how are you?" "Yeah, man, I'm good, I'm good; what about you?" The exchange was uncomfortable, like when you and your new partner run into an ex. Only in this case, no one was anyone's ex—at least, not yet.

♡ ～ ♡ ～ ♡

A few years before I started dating Jaedon and Luke, I had a nonmonogamous fling with another man I accidentally fell in love with— Jesse. (I've mentioned him before; he was the guy who gave me that "I love you" note.) I bring this up because after Jesse and I broke up, I learned one of the most important lessons about polyamory I would ever learn, and it carried over to all my relationships thereafter.

Jesse broke up with me, and I was totally crushed—but I'd assured him that I would care about him no matter what shape our relationship needed to take, and I was going to keep my promise, period. I invited him to dinner every week. I told him about the shows I was in at the comedy theater. I went to his house when he invited all his friends over—even though I knew the new girl he was sleeping with would be there—because I was his friend, and this "conscious uncoupling" was going to be different than all the other breakups I'd had in the past. It didn't matter that I hated him.

I hated him and hated him and hated him—until I didn't. At some point, after dinners and movie nights and calls to his mother in Florida, I began to see Jesse as a different man who existed outside the context of my past relationship with him, and I enjoyed having him around. For example: He knew a lot about birds. He told me once about how he watched hummingbirds harvest spiderwebs to build their nests, and I couldn't think of anything more beautiful in the world. Over lunch, when it was just the two of us, Jesse would still tell me how sad he was.

In those moments, all I could think about was how much I wanted this person to be happy. In fact, in those moments, it was *all* I wanted.

And so, months after we broke up, I started to tell him that I loved him. And he said he loved me, too.

The next spring, Jesse prepared to work on a farm where his ex would also be working. I asked if they were back together. No, he said, his ex was seeing a woman now, and it seemed serious; but he still cared for her very much, and he was interested in seeing what would happen over the summer they spent together.

It surprised me that I didn't feel jealous. I am, historically, a very jealous person. I like to have control over the people in my life, even if I don't like to admit it. I loved Jesse so much, and it surprised me that I didn't want to possess him. But I found myself hoping that things would go well with this woman, that maybe some healing could take place.

I was actually discovering something very important about poly-amory: it's not so much about letting the people you love sleep around and attend exotic sex parties with frisky, leather-clad barmaids (clearly I know nothing of that world, as I'm pretty sure the barmaid thing went out of style in the 1980s); it's not really about letting the people you love do anything. It's more about allowing yourself to let go. In releasing whatever possession you think you have over another person, you give yourself permission to not worry about it. Mistrust is a heavy burden to have to lug around all the time.

Luke never asked me to stop seeing Jaedon; he never said that he wanted more of my time or attention. He never complained about Jaedon or said that he felt jealous. When I asked him about jealousy, he said there was something about "coming into an open relationship as the new guy" that made him feel more guilty than jealous. To that end, it bears noting that there were definitely other reasons Jaedon and I decided to discontinue our physical romance. I firmly believe that relationships don't end because new people come along to break them up; people come along to break them up because something else in the relationship is already off. Jaedon and I were in fundamentally different places in our lives. Nevertheless, it was true that I had fallen in love with Luke, though I still felt just as much in love with Jaedon as I ever did.

After a year of dating and dating other people and processing the dating of other people, Jaedon and I decided to "transition out of a primary partnership." This was different from a regular breakup in that we didn't fight about it, really. It was more like a formal, peaceful secession agreement cautiously signed by leaders of a formerly united country. When I tell people about this now, I say that it was easy, that it went off without a proverbial hitch. But, of course, that's not true. We may not have fought, but we did spend hours and hours sitting in parked cars and on couches talking about feelings. I cried a *lot.* Human beings don't like change, and even though I could theoretically transition out of a relationship with Jaedon, actually not being with him broke my heart.

For example, Jaedon and I had started watching *Twin Peaks* together, and we hadn't finished it. We'd agreed early on—as couples who are adopting serial television watching habits will do—not to watch it independently of each other. Had this been a clean, normal, textbook breakup, all bets would have obviously been off around the subject of watching more episodes of *Twin Peaks.* But this was not that. Hanging out together during this transitional time was painful for both of us, but we were mutually obtuse about our insistence on staying friends. So did I continue to save *Twin Peaks* for my non-boyfriend-but-still-friendly-friend Jaedon?

Although this was confusing (understatement), it was also at the center of my interest in polyamory. Where are the lines between "romantic partner" and "friend"? I'm interested in a kind of fluidity—love among friends and partners and family members that resists definition and distorts traditional ideas about priority. Once, on a trip home to Portland from college with one of my long-term, monogamous boyfriends (Rory), I texted Jessica (remember Jessica?) to hang out. I asked her if it was okay if Rory came along, and she said, "I'd rather just spend some quality time with you." At first I thought that this was an absurd request. "If you're going to love me, you're going to have to love him," I thought. I believed I was going to be with this guy forever; I wanted my high school best friend to know who he was. Annoyed, I acquiesced, and we met for jam scones at the shopping center between our houses. In fact, we spent three hours together; I lost track of time with Jessica, just as I had done when we were in high school, before there were any boyfriends, when our time was informal and easy and unwound in the most comfortable and pleasurable way time can.

Prioritizing my friendship with Jessica over my relationship with Rory felt unnatural. I'd grown up believing that romantic partnership trumped all the other friendships there were. As a result, I often got frustrated with my romantic partners for not being able to provide what my friends could—long, bubbly conversations about Ben Folds Five; long, serious conversations about childhood emotional trauma; or honest-but-friendly advice about what to wear to a costume party.

It took a while for me to understand that I could have both kinds of relationships in my life; the important thing was that I actively prioritize each of them.

My relationship with Jaedon gave me so much. He was interested in academic theories, stories, and philosophies, which reminded me of my family and my childhood dinner-table conversations. He and I both had experience in the professional performing scene (mine was mostly in comedy; his was in Greek theater). He listened well. We both taught at the same school, so we could discuss other teachers and class sizes and administrative changes. He was kind to me, and he often said just what I needed to hear when I felt small. I believe— based on the letters we exchanged and the late nights we spent unable to stop talking—that I gave a lot to Jaedon, too.

It was painful to lose the things that came with our relationship. When you're in a partnership with someone, you tend to default to your partner when the weekend rolls around and it's time to make plans. Partnerships allow for you to order a whole pizza on a Wednesday night and eat half of it without experiencing any guilt. I liked sleeping next to Jaedon. He had a very sweet, curled-up way of sleeping that reminded me of videos of kittens. I liked sitting side by side with him, writing in my journal and listening to the Bad Plus. I liked his parents, and I liked visiting his family in Connecticut. These were activities specific to our partnership—perks that ran out when we downgraded to the less intense "friendship only" package.

The loss was also illuminating, because it helped me see how deeply and naturally I had fallen into familiar patterns of exclusivity. (See the paragraph above.) I had wanted polyamory to mean that I could float between partners fluidly, loving each person differently but equally, varying my respective intensity with the weather. You know how when you're watching someone who's very skilled at yoga do some kind of crazy, upside-down pretzel pose, it looks sort of easy? Like, the person is smiling and maybe their eyes are closed, and you think to yourself, "I bet I could do that." But then you go to actually try the pose and don't even know where to start. You bend your legs and fold in your belly, but no matter what you do, you end up a pancake on the floor. I assumed that entering into a polyamorous relationship would be relatively easy; I understood the logic of it and saw other people doing it. But faced with its reality, I fell. At first, I was too used to the motions of making big promises ("I'll be with you forever") and claims ("You're the only one I really love") that I couldn't keep and that weren't completely true. I knew how to make a person happy in the short term, but I was unprepared for what it meant to be honest about my feelings around a relationship all the time ("I need some space, to tell you the truth"; "I want to spend Saturday with Hannah"). Polyamory asks its participants to be self-aware and to constantly examine their priorities. While that's exhausting, I find it also to be a beautiful exercise in honesty—an exercise that, with time, becomes natural practice.

Ultimately, I decided to not finish *Twin Peaks* without Jaedon. Friends watch TV together all the time, and I hoped there would be a time in our lives when we would be able to pick it up again.

One of the greatest gifts of my partnership with Jaedon was the absence of anger when the relationship changed. There was sadness, and pain, and hurt—the normal stuff that comes with change. But I think we both left the partnership unscarred. Not unchanged, but without the trauma, the scabs, the ugly remnants most breakups leave behind. We still talk on the phone once every few months or so.

♡ ⌇ ♡ ⌇ ♡

Three months into my relationship with Luke, he invited me to run the children's section of the French festival he coordinated. First of all, the guy *coordinated a French festival.* I'm not a Francophile or anything, but it's very attractive to me when people are capable of coordinating things. I find it difficult to coordinate an outfit; there's no way I could coordinate a whole festival. I'd agreed to volunteer because I wanted to spend all my free time with Luke. We stood in his dim kitchen and filled water balloons for "the storming of the Bastille"—apparently a lighthearted annual fixture of the festival.

My job was to run the Bastille, or, as it was colloquially known, the "kids' area." We covered a play structure in the local park where the festival took place with white parchment paper and poured watered-down tempera paint into plastic cups. The kids at the festival were supposed to transform the play structure into a castle over the course of the day with paint and imagination. I tried to implement rules around this activity for approximately twelve minutes before giving in to the impossibility of the task. The dozens of children—some as young as two years old, some as impossible-to-boss-around as eleven—reduced my sorted paint system to anarchy, combining all the colors into a massive brown blob in the grass. They did this with a gleeful recklessness that I could only respect. Granted, had I been a parent of any of those kids, I would have been *pissed* about how the Bastille was managed. No one escaped unscathed.

Luke, however, thought everything was going just the way it was supposed to. He loved the brown blobs of paint; he loved the messy, screaming kids. "You're doing great," he said, and then he disappeared to wire the sound system on a small festival stage nearby. I saw him fuss with a convoluted nest of wires and watched as the singer on stage, who had been silenced by a useless microphone, suddenly heard her voice amplified. I heard her say to Luke, "Oh, thank God. You're an angel." I'm not completely sure why this was the moment I knew I loved Luke, but I think it had to do with his priorities (there's that word again): here was a person who was more interested in joy and fun and mess than he was in rules or order or neatness. At 5:00 p.m. he hauled plastic crates of water balloons to the play structure. He gave me about ten balloons; the rest went to the kids.

"I'm sorry about this," he said. "Sort of."

Everything after that was a swirl of candy-colored rubber explod-ing everywhere, and water in my nose canal. After it was all done, I couldn't stop thinking about the man who had put me in a position to spend a crazy-hot Saturday being attacked by thrilled children armed with water balloons.

But I didn't tell him. "I love you" freaks people out. Would he say it back? And remember: this was while I was still in a relationship with Jaedon. Did I have to tell Jaedon that I wanted to tell Luke that I loved him? I thought it would probably be prudent, but I didn't want to. So I held on to it for a few months, until the feeling of love was too much to bear. Like a true hero with guts of steel, I decided I would declare my love to Luke via Facebook Messenger:

> I want to tell you that I love you. I know that those are words relationships are scared of, but I do love you, and I also believe life is too short not to tell the people you love that you love them. I actually love you kind of a lot.

I immediately regretted sending this message. It wasn't the same as reading the cues over the course of a romantic night and feeling the feeling of "I love you" and saying it cinematically.

Within moments, Luke messaged back:

I LOVE YOU TOO!

I really do.

I was thinking about it last night.

I can't wait to say it out loud.

And then he added:

Also, are you trying to build some sort of case to show that people can be in happy/intimate relationships despite things like Tinder and Facebook Messaging?

He had a good point. I felt embarrassed about this then, but I'm glad for it now, because I have primary relationship documents that can be used in a research context. That's a big win for me. I also think I'm in a growing population of people who feel cooler, more articulate, and infinitely better at flirting in a text format than in person. I imagined that Luke imagined I was sitting at a chestnut desk wearing a beret and sipping one of those horrible tiny espressos cool people sip. (How do they even *do* that? An espresso is a *single sip*, period.)

Saying "I love you" changes everything. Maybe *that's* its real translation. "I love you," read as: "I want everything to change now." Like I said: it's worthwhile to constantly reevaluate the meanings of important words in order to get the most out of relationships. In our case, "I love you" allowed Luke to call me whenever he drove to Baton Rouge for work (which was often); it let me occasionally name him as my plus-one at events; it stretched the boundaries around what permissible Christmas presents were.

Six months later, after Jaedon and I had stopped seeing each other romantically and after Luke and I had spent hours discussing apartments and the possibility of someday getting cats, I rented a moving truck. I'd decided to go to the School of the Art Institute of Chicago, and Luke was coming with me.

Traversing the country in a sixteen-foot moving truck between New Orleans and Chicago required a lot—a lot of money, a lot of time packing and lifting and loading and unloading boxes, a lot of emotional energy, a lot of emotional time. When I say "emotional time," I'm talking about the way time expands inside the space of real work. The moving day was probably the longest one of my life.

I couldn't imagine doing any of this by myself. Luke drove the entire way; he pulled expertly into an Indian restaurant right outside Memphis at dinnertime, about halfway along the route. He remembered to pack the mattress and the wineglasses last, because he knew we would need only a bed and a glass of wine when we walked into our new apartment at close to midnight. Luke had found the apartment on the Internet, and he called the guy to secure it, and he'd spent the past several months taking daily virtual Google Maps strolls down our new street, so he knew right where the 7-Eleven was. I wasn't a damsel in distress here—I'd organized the route, and we'd needed my credit card to rent the truck—but it wasn't a one-person job.

This was not the first time I understood partnership. I'd felt this feeling with my roommates over the course of our cohabitation. There was always someone who could be at home when we needed to call a plumber; if one person was short with their rent, another person could make it up this month; when parents came to visit, the bathroom scrubbing and sink disinfecting could be divvied up. (That last one isn't really true. It should have been true, but Hannah always cleaned everything. I didn't really know how to clean until after I'd lived with

SOME JOBS WHEN YOU ARE MOVING

her and observed her for several years.) A lot has been said on the functionality of mutualism, but the greatest benefit is absolutely emotional. Partnership implies a support system that reveals itself in times of peril—like when Hannah and Derek peeled me off the floor in the wake of my breakup with Sam and put me to bed. And for the record: yes, it was difficult to leave Hannah and Derek and our weekly family dinners, but we'd recently had to move into a smaller house, and it was beginning to feel a bit too small for three people. (I did sob uncontrollably in the moving truck at hour thirteen, when it hit me just what I was leaving behind. Luke was patiently sympathetic. I still cry sometimes from missing Hannah so much.)

I had throbbing-cocoon syndrome. I was ready to move forward.

♡ ⌒ ♡ ⌒ ♡

The drive was a million hours long, and it was mostly past cornfields. Every once in a while there would be a big-seeming bird on an IHOP billboard, but it would invariably be something boring, like a crow. There wasn't a radio or a CD player in the truck. Luke put his intermittently working boom box in the front seat, and we listened repeatedly to the mixtapes he'd made me. We exhausted the topics of road food, the imminently imploding love lives of our mutual friends, and houseplants. Eventually, it was time for us to speak at some length about our relationship.

I decided to say that I didn't really want to be in any relationships outside my primary partnership with Luke. In retrospect, this was manipulative. When I said, "I'm satisfied with our relationship right now; I'm not going to pursue things with anyone else," I meant, "It would be an asshole move on your part to date other people, because I'm dedicated to you. At least for now. At least until something interesting comes along." I expected Luke to react to my proposal of monogamy-for-the-time-being with relief. "Oh, yeah, me, too. Good," he was supposed to say.

But Luke told me that that didn't sound like a polyamorous relationship to him.

And, of course, he was right. So we practiced. We continue to practice—usually sloppily, but somewhat consistently—to this day.

PART 6

Jealousy

I'm into the idea of polyamory, and I believe in it wholeheartedly. I'm in a polyamorous relationship with a person I really love and trust. But despite all that, I still get jealous. What do I do about my jealousy?

Versions of this question came up four times during a taping of a Dan Savage podcast Luke and I attended.

We leaned forward a little when those questions were asked. Savage sort of floundered with them, though. His answers ranged from "Jealousy is a normal emotion to feel in situations like these, and it's fine to feel that way as long as you don't act out because of it" to "I don't know, yeah, jealousy is hard." While a question like "What do I do when my boyfriend can't get an erection?" comes with an arsenal of sexy things to try and self-accepting phrases to repeat and practice, "What do I do when I'm jealous?" leaves most of us feeling a little uneasy.

When I talked on the phone with Savage, I asked him to extrapolate a little on the subject of jealousy. I hoped he would go on the record with some thoughts about what people who wanted to try polyamory but felt too jealous might do.

"Jealousy isn't necessarily this terrible thing," Savage told me. "It feels awful, but it doesn't have to destroy a relationship. Most people get jealous; I'm in an open relationship and I get jealous; Terry gets jealous; it's normal. What matters is the process of talking about that feeling, and different people have different capacities for handling it. If jealousy is a bomb that's just constantly going off, if it's going to

153

explode and hurt the relationship, hurt the people in your life, then polyamory may not be for you. But if jealousy is something you're able to defuse through communication and processing, then it can actually help your relationship."

David M. Buss, a self-proclaimed expert on the evolution of human sexuality, writes that jealousy is necessary. There's an underlying assumption in his book *The Dangerous Passion* that infidelity is terrible, and that participation in infidelity indicates that a person's love for "his mate" has faded. Buss does acknowledge polyamory in one paragraph of his book and quotes scholars and advocates for polyamory stating for the record that they think jealousy is bad. He quotes activist Kathy Labriola saying that jealousy is "the biggest obstacle to creating successful and satisfying open relationships."[1] But he ultimately asserts that people who commit themselves to polyamory are not really acknowledging the usefulness of jealousy. Jealousy can be used, for example, to prove to yourself that you're still emotionally committed to your mate. Jealousy indicates that the feeling of attachment still exists. Since humans have evolved to feel it, it must be useful.

Buss insists that because love and infidelity are universal parts of the human emotional landscape, then jealousy must also be. In *Sex at Dawn*, authors Christopher Ryan and Cacilda Jethá disagree: "Some behaviors that seem normal to contemporary people (and which are therefore readily assumed to be universal) would quickly destroy many small-scale foraging societies, rendering them dysfunctional."[2] The point here is that small groups of people trying to live together harmoniously might not be able to survive if seized in the clutches of jealousy. So how is it that tribes like these have continued to thrive? Ryan and Jethá say it is because people in those small tribes actually don't experience jealousy.[3] And how is *that* possible? They theorize that it's because they all sleep with one another regularly and nonmonogamously; so-called infidelity is therefore nonexistent.

We can't all live in little tribes in which no one knows who anyone's father is, so what are we Western city dwellers (and Facebook users) supposed to do? Do we have to accept jealousy as a natural part of all our romantic endeavors for the rest of our lovemaking lives?

We seem to have an easier time handling jealousy in other aspects of our existence; for example, Ryan and Jethá mention that firstborn children often feel jealous when a younger sibling comes along.[4] I relate to that: when my sister, Alexis, was born, I tried to put her in the garbage can to get rid of her. (It didn't work.) My mother constantly reminded me that I was just as special as Alexis and that she would always love us both exactly the same amount, but in different ways, because we were different people. And by the time I was four, I believed that. Why shouldn't this tenet hold true in romantic partnerships, too?

But sometimes it's not so easy. Jealousy is tricky; the truth is probably somewhere in between Buss's idea that jealousy is evolutionarily advantageous and Ryan and Jethá's suggestion that jealousy is mostly a learned trait, taught to us through social conditioning. Maybe musing about the evolution of a complex emotion like jealousy is ultimately not all that useful. "A more meaningful question," Deborah Anapol writes, "might be, is it possible to overcome jealousy and its destructive effects, or does choosing polyamory imply signing up for a lifetime of jealous agony and melodramatic crises as some people fear?"[5]

The best advice I've found about jealousy is likewise not at all simple. It's in a book called *The New Intimacy*, in which author Dr. Ron Mazur says that jealousy doesn't have a single definition but instead, like love, has a spectrum of versions.[6] Depending on which form of jealousy you're experiencing, there are a range of solutions or things to try. For instance, you might experience what Mazur has dubbed possessive jealousy, fear jealousy, competition jealousy, ego jealousy, or exclusion jealousy.[7] What—you don't know the difference between those five jealousy types? Lucky for you, I've created a reference chart on the next page, complete with possible solutions.

Luke and I talk about jealousy all the time; these discussions are a central part of our relationship.

But it wasn't always that way. Let's back up a bit, to right before Luke and I moved to Chicago. After Jaedon and I transitioned out of our romantic partnership in February, Luke and I enjoyed a bit of a honeymoon period. Had we not told everyone we were polyamorous, our relationship would have looked a lot like a monogamous one. The only thing that separated it from out-and-out monogamy during that time, really, was the *possibility* that something would change.

And then something did change the summer before we moved to Chicago, when I met Bob (with whom, you'll remember, I was extremely sexually compatible) at a summer camp where we were both counselors. Bob taught videography and I taught creative writing. I already knew of Bob and his artwork. He had done a set of "wigglegrams"—film photographs taken with a four-lens camera that were turned into 3-D animated gifs—for the online literary magazine I edited. Later that summer, I ran into him at a crawfish boil on the lake, and he introduced himself. He was wonderfully tall and had on an airbrushed T-shirt. I thought he was cute; before he left, he said he hoped he would see me around.

And now, here we were at summer camp—a place where crushes historically snowball in all the best ways.

On the second day of camp we were both placed in a small group tasked with making a video about how to not damage paintbrushes. We both took this project unnecessarily seriously. I went home and wrote a script that I hoped Bob would think was funny. (Bob was just so *cool*. He made very hip art. He'd recently produced a music video for Big Freedia.) The script required a real person to play the paintbrush, while another real person picked her up and dipped her hair in real paint and then painted with her. We found a waifish intern with the palest straw-colored hair and a strong-armed counselor to perform in the film. Bob spent hours filming takes. The four-minute video took an entire day to shoot.

TYPE of JEALOUSY	Possessive Jealousy	Fear Jealousy
LOOKS LIKE	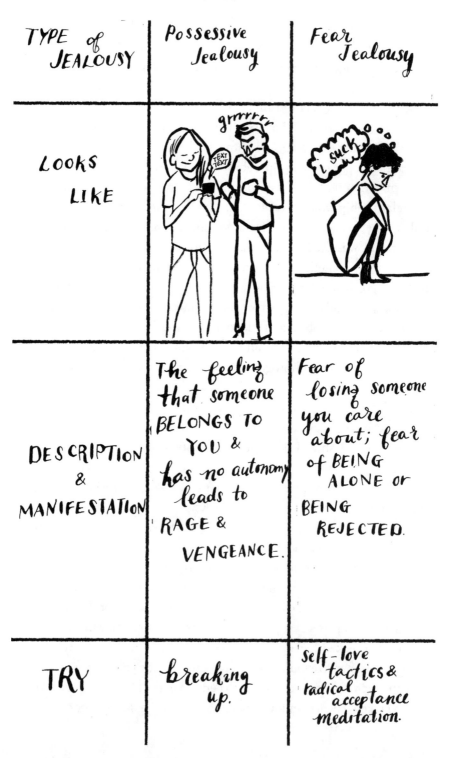	
DESCRIPTION & MANIFESTATION	The feeling that someone BELONGS TO YOU & has no autonomy leads to RAGE & VENGEANCE.	Fear of losing someone you care about; fear of BEING ALONE or BEING REJECTED.
TRY	breaking up.	self-love tactics & radical acceptance meditation.

After we had the initial footage, I sat in Bob's classroom to record a few voice-overs. This was three days into our friendship, and it had become clear to me that I was flirting with Bob. I thought that Bob was probably flirting back. In the classroom, I dropped my favorite flirtatious line: "Tell me a secret."

I expected Bob to pause, because that's what people usually did. They usually looked intrigued by the question; ordinarily, a person who has been asked this question responds with flirtatious follow-ups: *What kind of secret? Like a secret I've never told anyone before?* Bob didn't ask the follow-up questions, though. Instead he said, "Here's a secret: I didn't have sex for the first time until I was twenty-one." And then he launched into a sordidly detailed version of the story of the time he lost his virginity.

I recognized this as a flirtatious countermove. You don't tell a person about your sex life unless you want them to think about you having a sex life. I listened; I giggled at strategic moments; I told him the story of how I lost *my* virginity. The next day, in the afternoon, Bob kissed me in my writing classroom. And it was exciting. But also, it was awful.

It was awful because I knew it was going to upset the ease of the nice, functionally monogamous relationship I'd fallen into with Luke. Since Jaedon had left the picture, we'd never really discussed any rules; the only thing that we'd been explicit about was that we should tell each other if anything physical happened with anyone else. I think, though, that we both believed that nothing physical was going to happen with anyone else for a long time. We were very in love, and we got to tell all our friends we were polyamorous, so not only were we in love but we also appeared to be a little cooler than we really were.

In July, when Bob kissed me in my writing classroom, I felt the initial flutter of a first kiss (it was a *good* first kiss; just the right amount of tongue), but then came the sharp stomach plunge that accompanies the knowledge that you've done something you shouldn't have. After camp, I contemplated telling Luke about the kiss with Bob, and then decided to wait. What if it was a one-time kiss? Luke didn't have to know about a onetime kiss.

Luke came over to make dinner with me that evening. We liked to make coconut-milk curry—it was easy, because you could just throw lots of things into one pot, and the coconut milk made it taste good no matter what. As I chopped sweet potatoes at the kitchen table, my phone buzzed. It was a text message from Bob, I was sure of it. I checked: it was a text message from my sister, Alexis. Well, but, it *could* have been from Bob. I couldn't stop thinking about how Bob was probably going to send me a text message. I was unable to concentrate on anything else. In my distraction, I cut the tip of my finger with the chef's knife.

It was more like a blurt, an inadvertent sound rising up from my belly that I couldn't keep from coming out of my mouth.

"Oh. Okay," Luke said. He seemed unsurprised. I'd told Luke about Bob. I hadn't told him we were mutually flirtatious, exactly, but I'd told him that I met Bob. And then I told him that I thought Bob was funny. And then I told him that Bob had texted me *the funniest dog picture* last night. And from there, Luke had probably pieced together that maybe we were starting to flirt with each other.

Luke had been chopping zucchini, and he shoved the slices haphazardly into the already-bubbling saucepot while I went to get a Band-Aid. "Well, that's cool. To tell you the truth, I'd been thinking about maybe trying to hang out with Kat." Kat was the girl Luke had met years ago in New Orleans in a stupidly perfect way. (The short version is that he saw her from a distance one afternoon during his first weekend in New Orleans, essentially wished for her, set out to find that kind of girl in the evening, took home someone beautiful, and realized, upon seeing this evening girl's sunglasses, that the evening girl *was* the afternoon girl. Luke tells it better than this, but for reasons I'm sure you can guess, it's not my favorite story.) She was the kind of beautiful that defies description.

"Oh! Yeah. Yeah, you should! You should totally ask out Kat. On, like, a date." I didn't want Luke to ask Kat on a date. I understood that this was hypocritical of me, but I also didn't think this was an even playing field. I mean, I'd been kissed, innocently, by a tall, gawky camp guy, *one time*! And here Luke was talking about getting back together (basically) with his gorgeous and perfect ex-girlfriend. Was he seriously thinking that these were comparable situations?

"I mean," I added, "I don't really think this thing with Bob is going to happen again, you know. I think this was really the only time. But, yeah! If you want to go out with Kat, go out with Kat! Yeah. I'm not going to stop you."

"Cool," Luke said. "Shit, we forgot the red onion."

At this point, it's unfair to make assumptions about what Luke was thinking. What I *thought* Luke was thinking was, "Oh, good, I've been waiting and waiting for Sophie to make the first move with some loser guy so I can finally have the opportunity to get back together with my gorgeous ex-girlfriend whom I am still totally in love with." I continued to think that this was what Luke had been thinking until I began writing this chapter. Luckily, because Luke and I live together now, I was able to ask him about it.

I asked him one morning when he was drinking coffee and reading the *New York Times Magazine* and I was buried in books from the library about jealousy. (Spoiler alert—they all sort of say the same thing: "Jealousy is normal, but you can fight it!")

"Don't get distracted by my typing," I said, transcription fingers ready. "Be as brutally honest as you can be."

"Well, I guess I felt like I knew it. I felt like there was this confirmation that all my fears were coming true; but also that I knew in my brain that it wasn't that big a deal and that it would be okay. But I didn't *feel* that. There was just this thing where I saw this relationship with Bob coming but you kept denying it, and I felt like it was so obvious. I guess I felt that at some level you had been a little dishonest."

"Hmmm. Okay. Interesting." I was trying my best to mimic a therapist and not to seem personally invested in this conversation. "And then, when I told you about Bob, you told me you were going to ask out Kat."

"I did? Okay, yeah, I guess I did."

"Did you do that because you wanted me to be jealous?"

I pause here to note the following objective fact: Luke is a saintly person. I don't know if I've adequately depicted him that way, but he really is. Like, he's always giving up his Saturdays to do odd jobs for our (also odd) next-door neighbor. He loves to put up shelves for Stanley's cowboy boots or South American relics, and he brings leftover soup to Stanley's house when we have it. Luke is also the kind of person who gets giddy when you ask him to help you move. He's there on time and has coffee for everyone and stays after everyone else has left to make sure you don't need anything moved around.

Here's another perfect example.

One time as I was watching a pair of cardinals at our bird feeder, I saw Luke (who had been picking up something from the drugstore) lock his bike to the No Parking sign outside our house and then run down the street to help an old lady carry her bags inside, like a kid in a 1950s advertisement for the Boy Scouts. He made three trips and then waved good-bye to her and came home and made me a cup of chamomile tea just because he thought I'd like one. The clincher here is that he never told me that he helped the old woman. I've only ever helped old women in order to tell people that I helped them. I recently signed up to volunteer at a soup kitchen, told every person I encountered that day that I had signed up to volunteer at a soup kitchen, and then canceled my volunteer spot the next day.

I add all this so you'll understand why I assumed that Luke, saintly saint that he is, would tell me that *of course* he didn't want me to be jealous! He was interested in going on a date with Kat, but he knew that he wasn't going to leave me for her or anything, and he was going to take this opportunity—which opened up because I made out with someone else—to go on a date with a person he deeply cared about. And yet, when I asked Luke if he had wanted me to feel jealous, he faltered.

"Um . . . hmm. Maybe?" This threw me.

"Really!" I said. I felt like a scientist who, after months of false starts, had discovered that all mouse bodies react badly to sugar. What I mean is that if there was ever a person who was capable of entering into his first polyamorous relationship without allowing jealousy to dilute his compassion, it was Luke. That Luke, of all people, became a tiny bit malicious once jealousy was added to the mix confirmed for me that jealousy has the capacity to make monsters of us all.

So, the summer before we moved to Chicago, while I made out with Bob at a rich kids' camp, Luke went on one date with Kat. He bought her a fourteen-dollar drink that was basically an alcoholic sno-ball. (A sno-ball is like a snow cone, but the ice is more finely ground, and New Orleanians don't like it when you compare the two.) Then they went to Muriel's restaurant, which is a witchy and mysterious building full of burgundy crushed velvet and gold tassels. They sat out on the balcony to talk. They made out in the Séance Lounge—which is a definitely haunted but nevertheless sexy space that no one ever goes to on the top floor of the restaurant. And I know all this because I asked Luke to tell me everything, and he very calmly did.

I went on lots and lots of dates with Bob, most of which I did not share with Luke. Mostly the "dates" were hooking up in different parts of camp. We had this map of the camp, and when we made out somewhere new, we marked the map with a sticker. Sometimes kids would see the map and ask what the stickers were all about, and we said that those were the places where we knew for a fact there were ghosts. I don't know about you, but nothing heats up a relationship for me faster than openly lying to children.

"Hooking up" is one of those ambiguous terms that could mean anything from holding hands to penetrative sex (a wide range, I know). A 2011 study conducted by Amanda Holman at the University of Nebraska–Lincoln sought to define the word, but after interviewing 274 college students, she found that there was no real consensus.[8] It's a term that annoys me because it seems to imply a lack of emotional intimacy; it's ambiguous on purpose to keep a loose framework around what might or might not happen on an alcohol-fueled night when one or both people get physical for the sake of "fun."

I'm using the term "hooking up" here because I don't want to incriminate myself as doing anything specifically naughty after hours at a summer camp for children. (The children had all gone home, just to be clear.)

Sometimes I drove Bob home in my Volvo sedan, which didn't have a working speedometer or a driver's side mirror. I took twisty routes that didn't get us back to his house as quickly as possible. In the car, I told Bob stories about my greatest fears and shared my deepest secrets. In the front console of the car were stacks of mixtapes Luke had made me. Bob picked them up and asked why I had so many tapes when it was not 1993. I told him Luke was a mixtape wizard. Bob was enthusiastic about that and wanted to listen to the tapes. "Luke seems like such a cool guy; I hope we can spend some time together," he said.

Once, Bob invited me to come into his house with him. He lived in a very inexpensive house in an expensive neighborhood. I didn't completely understand the story of the house, but it was something like this: the person who owned it didn't want to bother with finishing it properly (it was a huge house), and so this owner let a bunch of people live there and pay cheap rent as long as the people didn't complain about how there were no doors or how you could see the insulation in the walls or how the entire house seemed to be slightly rotting.

Bob had a regular cast of five roommates, and the house was big enough to accommodate any number of traveling guests at any given time. There were Polaroid pictures of naked women on the walls in the entry hallway; the kitchen was twice the size of my entire house, but it was crawling with cockroaches and geckos that came in through the ample holes in the ceiling. Getting to Bob's room involved going through a bit of a labyrinth; I couldn't find my way back to it after I went to the bathroom. (The bathroom didn't have a door. You had to knock on the door frame before you went in so you didn't walk in on anyone.) In the summer, when the sticky heat in New Orleans is all but unbearable, Bob put a huge, portable air conditioner in his room to keep it cool, but I still found the space intolerably hot. It seemed like a joke that he had a comforter on his bed—as though he didn't throw it off every night so he could get as much of his bare skin up next to the AC as possible.

Bob and his roommates recently had to move out of that house

They put everything they didn't want out on the sidewalk.

I couldn't live in a house like this. That was the first thing I thought when I went inside. It wasn't because of the holes in the walls, or because I didn't believe I could stay alive without a properly working air conditioner; it was that the house was too big, and the people who lived there didn't have any real control over it. It was too big to collaboratively clean or decorate. I didn't see how anyone could ever bring themselves to scrub the stovetop, for example, because the stovetop was such a tiny corner of such a gargantuan kitchen that scrubbing it seemed futile; it would make no real difference in the way the kitchen looked. People in that house stayed up late and went out a lot and did bright, colorful, all-night projects. (In New Orleans, "doing colorful projects" is a typical pastime and may include but is not limited to: creating a Mardi Gras float out of papier-mâché, sewing a sequined costume by hand, or spray painting a bunch of plants neon colors.) The house was cooler than I was, and I had no real interest in being the kind of cool that was required by the house. I liked my immaculate

refrigerator and my roommates Hannah and Derek, who got frustrated
if you didn't clean the cast iron skillet enough.

Inside Bob's house, all my fears about a relationship with Bob somehow ruining my relationship with Luke dissipated. Bob was a free
spirit, and he wasn't going to lock me into a monogamous or primary
sort of partnership. Something about his house articulated this better than his words ever could. We made out on his bed, on top of the
superfluous comforter.

At the end of the summer, lying on the ground in Bob's video classroom at camp, he told me he loved me. It was one of the most lovely
"I love you"s I had ever heard. It reminded me a lot of the Jesse "I
love you": an "I love you" without strings; an "I love you" that carried
no real implication or baggage. The words meant exactly what they
meant: he loved me. There was no reason not to say it, because there
was nothing more beautiful than the capacity one human being has to
love another human being. I said, "I love you, too."

Sometimes, in movies, when people say "I love you," they act kind
of sad. They act like using this phrase is a sort of tragic concession, as
if underneath is, "I've tried not to love you, because I'm aware that I'm
not supposed to, and that for some reason my loving you is going to
damage our livelihoods, but damn it, I can't help it, I can't fight it, and

now that I've said it, I know that everything will be totally different." Bob's and my "I love you" exchange was the opposite of that. Nothing changed at all, except that there was now a new addition to our vernacular. It was like he had cut up strawberries to put in my cereal.

Saying "I love you" to Bob did not change the way I felt when I said "I love you" to Luke. This confirmed for me something that I had always suspected: love is not the same as waffles. A person does not possess a finite amount of love that they must divide among the people in their lives. When a person gives love to another person, it doesn't mean that there's less to give to yet another person down the line. With waffles, if you have six, you can either give one person all six or you can give one person three and another person three, but you can't give both people six. That waffle scenario would suck either way, because at the end of the day you've given all your waffles away, and what are *you* supposed to eat for breakfast?

on second thought,

I'm not physically capable of sharing waffles.

As the summer wound down and Luke and I prepared to move across the country together, Bob told me he was sad I was leaving. I was sad to leave him, too.

Bob and I stayed together on a long-distance basis for a long time, talking on the phone every few weeks and sending each other long emails. Our conversation began to shift a bit; we stopped talking so much about strange and private sexual fantasies or deep and dark secrets from our past and started talking more about video games from the 1990s that we both still liked to play or the logistics of scheduling. It wasn't that the conversation was any less engaging or enjoyable; it was just more familial. That happens over time. It's nothing to mourn.

Recently, Bob told me he'd fallen in love with someone else. My initial reaction to that news was strange for me: I felt really, genuinely happy for him. This was what the polyamorous community calls "compersion," and they talk about it like it's buried treasure or a secret elixir hidden in a forbidden temple.

"Compersion" is a term that's used to mean the emotion opposite of jealousy; it's a feeling of joy or pleasure that comes from a lover experiencing happiness in a new relationship.

Now that I've experienced it wholeheartedly, I understand the appeal. Compersion feels great. It feels like getting a free root-beer float.

I think Luke has started to feel it, too. For instance, I recently went to visit Bob. In the lead-up to my trip, Luke asked me how I felt about it:

This conversation was very cool. We congratulated ourselves for having it. In the back of my mind, I wondered how truthful any of this was. Was it really likely that my partner of two years was actually excited for me to go have sex with my other boyfriend? If you'd posed the question to me a decade ago, I would have laughed at you. But I decided to believe that Luke was happy for me in that moment. Luke is not a dishonest person; there really wasn't any reason for him to lie.

The Bob visit was great. We saw movies and had sex and ate floppy pizza slices and had sex and had sex and swam in a private pool. And we had really, seriously wonderful sex. That was the main thing. The sex.

Then I came back from the Bob visit, and I told Luke some of the details of the visit, and guess what: he wasn't that happy to hear them. He even used the J-word, and my faith in compersion was shaken. But at least I was happy for Bob and his other new girlfriend, right? (I didn't meet Bob's girlfriend when I visited; she happened to be out of town that weekend. From what Bob tells me, though, they spend almost every night together and go on trips and play with puppies together. It seems like a very serious, very healthy relationship from here.)

Then Bob stopped calling and stopped responding to my emails, and I recognized this as hard-core falling-in-love behavior—but this time he wasn't falling in love with me. I'd been relegated to a backup activity, an item on a to-do list. I wanted to be happy that Bob was happy. I could logic myself into something that seemed sort of like happiness. I could text Bob "I'm happy for you" and mean it—but when he didn't respond for four days, I found myself crying about it in a bathroom on an Amtrak train.

Once, while I was at a conference in Los Angeles, Luke went on a date with someone he matched with on Tinder. When he left to go on the date, I felt shitty about it. The anthropological thing to do, I decided, was to write about this date and my feelings around it as it was happening. (In other words, I needed an excuse to obsessively think about my boyfriend while he was on a date and frame it in a productive way; I was going to think about it anyway.) Here's what I wrote (and subsequently illustrated, for effect):

I'm writing this while my boyfriend, Luke, is on a date with another woman. I know the other woman's name, but I don't know much else about her—except that she's the kind of woman who would consider going on a date to a zoo.

Going on a date to a zoo is a thing I would never do, because I feel depressed looking at the lethargic animals eating dead fish next to fake rocks. When I was nine, on the day I decided I hated zoos, I saw a turtle swimming in a glass box no bigger than a loaf of bread, with no rocks or anything to sit on if he got tired. Almost nothing is more gruesome than the reality of a confused and innocent animal forced into a life of evident torture for the supposed pleasure of cotton candy–eating children.

Luke has wanted to go on dates with new people lately. He told me this last week over a small basil pizza we were sharing in a crowded bar. It was our first date in a long time, because we're both busy and have inverse schedules. When we have time off together, we usually bike five minutes to the bird sanctuary near our apartment to walk in silence (or sometimes I try to sing silly songs to make the birds feel more comfortable). Luke likes to fill his hands with birdseed and stand stock-still, because he can get chickadees to land on his fingers that way. We chose our apartment in part because of its proximity to this bird sanctuary, which is located on an abandoned army base that's now known, wonderfully, as the Magic Hedge. We like to go at all times of year, because the landscape has a tendency to change in ways you don't expect. Once we went when it was six degrees outside. I opened up a milkweed pod in my hand and watched the seeds flow out and blend into the snow.

Those don't count as dates, though, because I can wear sweatpants and no eyeliner, and we're together but we're also alone, meditating on the space and feeling the perfect freedom one feels when there are no walls and no one around to entertain. Sometimes we go get tacos, but that's almost always because we only have peanut butter in the fridge.

So if you don't count the trips to the bird sanctuary or the times we got tacos, this was our first date in three weeks. We had ice cream first, and then this fancy brick-oven pizza. I even ordered a drink with gin in it, which is unusual for me, because if I'm going to spend money to consume a lot of calories, I'm going to do it on something made of bread. Later, we were going to go see Zootopia at the expensive, trendy movie theater across the street. I was so pleased to be on this date; it felt like the kind of outing I assumed marriage counselors would urge their clients to go on. I was not pleased, however, when Luke said he'd been wanting to go on dates with new people.

I tried to appear pleased, though. After all, I was the one who'd insisted on a polyamorous relationship when we met a little over a year ago, and though Luke proved to be very into the idea of polyamory, I was the one who had another boyfriend in New Orleans, and Luke did not. In other words, Luke had quite a bit of credit in his dating-other-women account. He absolutely deserved to want to do it.

At the pizza place, I thought hard about the corners of my lips and forcibly willed them upward; I took a casual sip of my gin thing in a way that implied I was doing great. But in truth, I was irrationally angry that Luke would bring such a thing up on our date—or that he would bring such a thing up at all—or that such a thing could ever, in any universe, be what he wanted. "Oh, yeah?" I said. "That's great!" I always say "that's great" when I'm feeling jealous. It's what I said when my best friend told me she'd lost a lot of weight, and it's what I said when my coworker was going to have her short story published in Tin House.

"I just think that if we're going to be polyamorous, we should really be polyamorous. The longer we go not being functionally polyamorous, the less I believe it." I told him that I understood. I'll reiterate: I did understand. But that didn't lessen my impulse to throw my ice water at him.

We talked a little more about it. Was he talking to anyone? Yes, he'd found someone he liked on Tinder recently, and they'd been negotiating a date. (My brain said, "WHAT?! You've been talking to her FOR LONG ENOUGH to ALREADY BE NEGOTIATING A DATE?!?!?! WHEN WERE YOU GOING TO TELL ME?!?!?!?!?! WERE YOU GOING TO WAIT UNTIL YOU WERE ON THE DATE AND THEN TEXT ME IN THE MIDDLE OF THE NIGHT, AFTER I'D STARTED WORRYING THAT YOU HAD DIED?!?!?!?!?") I said that was great.

He said yes, he was excited about it. I started wondering whether I wanted to know more about this girl. Did I want to see her picture or know what she did for a living? I wasn't sure. I stayed quiet. Then I launched into an argument about how I didn't want to see anyone else because I was afraid it would compromise our relationship, because I wasn't feeling like our relationship had been particularly strong lately, and I didn't want to ruin that by getting all excited about someone new. Luke said that that made sense. He was supposed to tell me that he felt the same way, and never mind, he would cancel with this girl; but instead he said, "That makes sense."

The horrible sick feeling lingered, even after we changed the subject. I thought about the whole Luke-dating-someone-else thing when we crossed the street to go to the movie theater, and when we were getting the tickets. It faded somewhere in the opening sequence of Zootopia. (It's a good movie.)

Later, I considered something I'd heard on a Buddhist podcast once. The person on the podcast said that every choice you make in your life and everything you're feeling ultimately comes from a place of love or from a place of fear. This is obviously a gross oversimplification. But whatever, let's go with it. (Oh, like your podcast choices are so much better.)

If we're thinking in terms of love and fear, I'm afraid not because I love Luke so much but because I'm afraid of losing something. I'm afraid because

Then I might lose him. There is nothing I want less in the world than to lose him. (Read: fear jealousy type.)

But, on the other hand, I'm always at risk of losing the things I love. That's part of what makes love so valuable: it's vulnerable. We all must know this, because there's nothing but evidence that it's true; but we also know, in some deeper part of ourselves, that the risk is worth the payoff.

Luke would not be going on a date with another girl if he didn't feel like the foundation of our relationship was pretty healthy. I mentally took stock of all Luke would lose if he dumped me. We lived together, so if he left, he would need to separate all his records from my records. Plus, we both had a copy of this obscure New Orleans record by a band called Why Are We Building Such a Big Ship. How would we know whose was whose? That in and of itself would be a logistical nightmare.

Luke watched me meet and date and fall in love with Bob, and he told me that the jealousy, which was at first unbearable, faded into real, bona fide compersion. Luke promised me that he would never, in any circumstance that he could imagine, break up with me because he met some other girl. Boys have made promises like that to me before, and they've broken them. But other boys (and girls!) have made promises like that to me and kept them.

Trust is a hard thing to rebuild. I cannot count the times that some wonderful person I know has said something like, "I find it very difficult to trust people ever since [person X] did [thing Y]." My own weakness is that I have trouble believing that anyone can love me when I'm sad. I have a lot of evidence that my sadness is a problem, that it should be hidden or buried. In elementary school, I got sent to the school counselor because my teacher was concerned that I showed "a disproportionate amount of sadness given my age." A year later I happened to find a note that I assumed someone in my class had passed to someone else; I noticed it in the recycling bin because it had my name on it. It was just one line: "Don't tell Sophie she always just cries about everything." When I found the note, I went and sat in the big bathroom on the fifth-grade end of the hallway and cried about everything.

I've cried in bed and at the dinner table; I've cried on the phone and while staring at the phone wishing it would ring; I've cried under every desk in our apartment; I've cried in the bathtub and on the bathroom floor and with my head collapsed on the closed toilet. I've cried about things I know how to talk about, but mostly I've cried about things I don't understand at all. Sometimes I scream when I cry. Sometimes I even punch Luke on the arm. I'm trying to tell you that I've done some next-level crying around this guy. And here's what Luke does, every time: he holds me as close as I will let him hold me and says "It's okay" or "I love you."

When I really think about it, I'm not worried about Luke. When the worry is gone, so is the jealousy.

When I gave this piece to my graduate school advisor to read over, she tried to be gentle, but eventually she came right out and said it:

"Well, it's true. I just don't feel jealous anymore. The jealousy is over," I told her.

"Okay. I believe you believe that. But I don't believe it, and no one else is going to believe it, because that's not how jealousy works."

I really wish that the version of myself who wrote about my jealousy drifting away into nothingness had been right. It would have made my life—and writing this book—a lot easier. But I didn't actually stop being jealous after writing a drawn-out, glorified journal entry about it in Los Angeles. Things with the zoo girl didn't go anywhere, but things with the next girl did. It was months later when Luke met her, and I'd been on dates with other people since the zoo girl, too. The next girl—I'll call her Melissa, because she's become too important a figure in our lives to be boiled down to a single quirk—is a person Luke really likes, and he shared with me a text he sent her in which he told her she was beautiful and amazing and funny. The jealousy came back, and the processing, and the conversations, and the pain, and all the rest of it.

To be fair, it was a little easier this time. But "a little easier" does not a utopic relationship make.

When I get really honest about polyamory with people, they aren't convinced that it's a really viable relationship model. A friend in my graduate program asked me over tea recently, "Is it really worth it? I mean, couldn't it be maybe better to just give up dating other people in order to feel more secure in the idea of your relationship lasting? Don't you think it's possible that monogamy is just less painful?"

And yes, it absolutely *is* possible. Like I said in the beginning of this book, I don't think polyamory is for everyone. I used that very line on my friend, actually.

"Yes," she said. "But do you *really* think it's right for *you?*"

I couldn't answer her at the time—which was terrifying, because I'd spent a lot of time building an identity around my polyamory. The thing that had to happen in order to change things for me—forever, I hope—was that I had to hit bottom with Melissa.

As Luke continued to date Melissa, I continued to feel terrible. I wasn't sure how much I wanted to know about the relationship, and the happier Luke seemed to be, the worse I seemed to feel. And there was a double arrow here—I didn't want to tell Luke how bad I was feeling because I was afraid it would make him annoyed with me, and then he wouldn't be attracted to me anymore, and then he would leave me for Melissa. Once, as we were walking home from the grocery store, he told me that he wanted to maybe go spend the night at Melissa's house. (She lived in a suburb of Chicago, so it was hard for them to visit each other; there was a superlong train ride involved.) I was so jealous and had so little compersion that I was almost incapable of lying about it. I spent all my free time alone stewing in my jealousy.

Eventually, I was bothered so much that I decided to reach out to Melissa. I messaged her on Facebook, telling her I wanted to get to know her better. When she didn't respond immediately, I was no longer only jealous, I was downright *angry*. This girl, I felt, should be dropping everything to talk to me so that my feelings could be quelled. A real low point arrived. I got *very* mad at Luke and listened to a lot of whiny-sad breakup music (the kind with a piano and a singer and nothing else) while riding the bus. When I tried to explain my anger to Luke, I didn't feel any better. He tried to tell me that his relationship with Melissa really wasn't that serious, and that I was, maybe, overreacting.

Tip: Never tell an angry person that she's overreacting. If things weren't ignited before, using the word "overreacting" will explode the situation beyond recognition.

And then, eventually, Melissa messaged me back. Sure, we could get to know each other better, she said. I asked her about her likes and dislikes. She asked me what I did with my free time. She told me about her childhood, and I told her about mine. For days, we messaged back and forth; the messages were sometimes paragraphs long, and I found myself telling her things that some of my best friends didn't even know. Eventually, we talked about love; we talked about our pasts; we talked about Luke. A week into our conversation, I noticed that the fire in my gut had died down. I actually liked Melissa. I thought Melissa really liked me, too, and it seemed that she had no interest in taking anything away from me. I closed my eyes and imagined Luke leaving for a weekend to hang out with Melissa and noticed that, for the first time since he'd met her, I felt pretty okay with that idea.

♡ ⌒ ♡ ⌒ ♡

As I was working on this book, I spoke to lots of people in polyamorous relationships, secretly hoping to find someone who had beaten the whole jealousy thing. As far as I know, there isn't a person out there who has it all figured out. Dan Savage, celestial being that he is, told me he still gets jealous sometimes. When I asked a woman in the Chicago polyamorous community, who throws sex parties and has two partners and talks about all of it with ease and excitement, if she feels less jealous than she did when she started with polyamory, she couldn't answer because she was laughing so hard.

Louisa Leontiades, a poly blogger who lives in Sweden, also acknowledged that jealousy never totally fades, but she, at least, was very reassuring. She told me that in time, her jealous tendencies had lessened. "In the beginning, I didn't realize I had huge holes in my self-esteem," she said. "I've had to do a lot of work on myself and my fear of abandonment, and that work has helped me become far less jealous. I still have those kicks, but now I've developed a better prefrontal cortex response to them."

Valerie White, a polyamorous woman in her early seventies, said that she still feels jealous, but she's learned a few coping strategies:

"When jealousy happens—and it will—it's incumbent upon everybody to cherish the person who's feeling threatened," White said. Jealousy, like all emotions that involve suffering, has to be honored and treated with love. It sounded so simple when she said it, but when I thought back to the times Jaedon told me he was jealous, I remembered that I didn't cherish him; instead, I was defensive. It was hard for me to take a step away from my ego when I felt like I was in trouble. It was hard to understand that the jealousy really didn't have much to do with me at all.

I was lucky with Luke and Melissa, because they both took the time to cherish me when I was feeling jealous. They both graciously stopped what they were doing with each other to pay attention to me and to let me see into their world. Melissa wasn't scary when I got to know her; she transformed from a major threat to another human being simply doing her best. And really—from the very bottom of my heart—going into the scariest reaches of my emotional reality with Melissa and coming out on the other side totally safe was one of the single most fulfilling experiences I've ever shared with another person.

Understanding the value of other people's emotions—all of them, and maybe even especially the ugly ones—is what polyamory is really all about. One of the great gifts of jealousy is that it gives us the opportunity to love each other even harder, to warmly greet the humanity in one another and—this is more difficult—the humanity in ourselves.

PART 7

Relationships without Borders

I don't know *exactly* what's going to happen in my relationship with Luke, and the beauty of polyamory is that we don't have to have a plan. I see myself having children, but I'm not totally attached to that idea. If we both met someone we wanted to live with, I would be open to that. I feel open to everything. I'm not the only one on earth who believes in polyamory, and there are plenty of people who have made it work for decades—living in multipartner households, raising children, and redefining "family" as circumstances require.

But as of now, I want to be a mother more than I want probably anything else in the world. In some ways, I feel embarrassed about this; a lot of younger folks in my circle of poly friends have decided that they definitely *don't* want children, and there's real liberation in that decision for them. I'm not a person who believes—even a little bit—that children complete a family, or that a woman's purpose in life is to procreate. But I like kids much more than I like adults, as I never emotionally matured beyond the age of seven. (As I read that back to myself, I realize that it may not be the best argument for my being in charge of another human life, but there it is.) More important, I want to take care of someone who I get to watch grow. My itch to be a parent was only confirmed when I was a teacher. The worst part of the day was when the kids had to go home.

The first time someone said to me, "Well, you can't be polyamorous and have kids, though, right?" I sort of stammered. Of course I could! Why couldn't I? And then I began to wonder—as you are maybe wondering—about the logistics of such a thing. I didn't know any poly people with kids. Maybe I was setting myself up for failure.

And so I went where one goes when one thinks something might be impossible: Google. And Google took me, wonderfully, to Louisa Leontiades.

Leontiades has two children, a girl and a boy, who are six and four, respectively. She's fairly well known in the UK for writing a memoir called *The Husband Swap*, which chronicles her journey with her now ex-husband into a polyamorous relationship with another couple. She publishes a wonderful blog and advice column, and she often tackles questions about raising children in a polyamorous household. In one of her blog posts about poly parenting, Leontiades acknowledges some of the difficulties of raising children while in multiple relationships: balancing needs, dealing with children's questions, and coping with the emotional impact of fluctuating relationships. She writes, "There are solutions—many of them tough to swallow—but that's what parenting is about: suddenly having to make the difficult choices and assuming a lot more responsibility than you ever thought your shoulders were ready for."[1]

Leontiades lives in Sweden with her "nesting partner," whom she refers to publicly as Morten. Morten is the father of Leontiades's two children, but they no longer have a sexual relationship. Leontiades has a boyfriend, who has an apartment in the city; and Morten has a girlfriend, who recently moved to Berlin. "Morten and his girlfriend have an open relationship, but they are less polyamorous in the sense that they're not looking for any long-term relationships," Leontiades told me. She and her boyfriend, on the other hand, also have an open relationship but are not interested in hookups. "It's a matter of preference," she said. She and Morten are still very close, though; they raise their children with a sense of community in mind, which Leontiades describes as being like a tribe. When Leontiades told her mother that she and Morten "had transitioned," her mother took it to mean that they'd split up. But Leontiades insists that they never actually split up; it's just that the nature of the relationship changed.

I wanted to know what it was like raising children in a nontraditional arrangement. I wondered if it worked any differently than the nuclear model. "For me, polyamory is a godsend to my kids," Leontiades said. All four of the people in Leontiades's love life have different jobs and lifestyles—one is a scientist, for example; another is a corporate executive—and they all have different national backgrounds. Her children, therefore, witness a "panoply of options" for what they could possibly grow up to be. "They have this wide range of influences; they have supported care, different role models," Leontiades said. She likes that her children won't ever feel boxed in by one way of life.

Valerie White also told me that having more than two parents was a major advantage in raising children. White, who is seventy-one and has been practicing polyamory for decades, co-parents fourteen-year-old twins with her partners Judy and Ken.[2] Ken is fifty-five and Judy is sixty; Ken and Judy have been seeing each other since 1979 and added Valerie to their relationship in 1994. While Valerie and Judy are each partnered with Ken and not with each other, they live happily together in one house. When Judy decided she wanted to have children, Valerie's daughter offered to let Judy use her eggs (Judy was having trouble getting pregnant on her own), so Valerie is technically the twins' grandmother, but is functionally another parent. And that's just what's going on in the house! All three parents have or have had secondary relationships with other people since they started living together. While it might sound complicated to you, to Valerie this model mostly makes sense—especially when it comes to raising children.

"When it's one baby, it takes a village; with twins, it takes a small metropolitan area," she told me, laughing. When the twins were babies, White tended to them at night while Ken and Judy slept. "I need less sleep, and I'm more resilient about going back to sleep when woken up," White said. "When they woke up, if they needed feeding, I would change them and then call Judy over the intercom. It was a great system." As she talked about it, I couldn't believe how nice it sounded to have more support in raising your children. I told White that I'd never thought about what it would mean to be able to raise a child in a community, and that it sounded really amazing. White, who had previously been married and had children before she entered into her relationship with Ken and Judy, told me that she couldn't understand why more people didn't raise their children like that.

"Way back when my oldest child was a baby and I lived in England, there were six moms who had kids at the same time. And during the day, two of the moms would look after all the babies for a few hours in the mornings while the other moms had a chance to go out. For the two of us, when one of the babies needed feeding, we just fed it. We just nursed it. Since then, I've heard from other women that the idea of somebody else nursing their baby made them feel intensely jealous, and they would feel like they were betraying their baby," White said. But for White, sharing that kind of responsibility was the most natural thing in the world.

This idea that what for some is uncomfortable is utterly natural to others is at the center of what makes polyamory so difficult for people to understand. We tend to want things to have a firm set of guidelines; if we follow the rules correctly, we'll be successful. Polyamory isn't like that at all. As Dan Savage reminded me over the phone, "no two polyamorous relationships are alike."

Savage has talked on his podcast about how polyamorous relationships are like snowflakes in this way. Monogamous relationships are all structured with the exact same rules: I love you, you love me, and we're not allowed to be with anyone else. Polyamorous relationships, on the other hand, are all uniquely structured to accommodate the people participating in them. No two of them are exactly alike.

There are a few common threads, though. To simplify a little, I've provided a guide to some of the most common types of polyamorous relationship structures:

While a lot of this terminology is still coalescing, nontraditional family structures like those described in the chart are really nothing new. Queer communities have been stretching the meaning of the word "family" for decades. I spoke to the artist Chuck Thurow, who's lived in a

TERM	Polycule
	An interconnected relationship network including more than two people.
LOOKS LIKE	VALERIE WHITE'S situation is a good example. Her primary lives with her & with another primary partner. They all live together.  They have all had other secondary partners
RELATED TERMS	triad, quad, or other geometric configurations! A triad is where three people are dating each other. A quad is often composed of two couples who are also dating each other. In a polycule, people in a triad or quad may have other, secondary partners. There are also V & N geometries

*Disclaimer:
The definitions of terms are subject to change at any time without warning.

Polyfidelity	Open Relationships
Multiple romantic relationships inside one closed group, where each person is primary partners with each other person.	Both/all parties have agreed to have other romantic relationships outside their own.
Five people live in a community together. They all have sex, they all consider each other equal partners, &they do not date outside their community. They may make a life commitment.	Sophie & Luke are dating, but they date other people, too.
triad, quad, and other geometric configurations also apply. Here, though, everyone is primary, and the relationship is closed. Also: group marriage, group relationships, and tribes.	kitchen table polyamory, where everyone in a relationship feels comfy sitting around a table together; and parallel polyamory, where secondary relationships are entirely separate from primary ones. Also: metamour, who is the partner of your partner.

multiperson household for most of his adult life. He and his first partner, Dale, each took on other partners; eventually, five men came to live in a house together, continuing to love one another regardless of sexual commitment. "Our whole ethos at that time was to smash the nuclear family model," Thurow said. "We came out strong when we created gay liberation. If anything, we were too strong on the other side. There was something wrong with you if you had a closed relationship." Thurow was trying to say that in his circle, everything *but* the norm was acceptable.

Thurow told me that the relationships he had with the men he lived with—all of whom have now passed away—were deep and rich, and ultimately had little to do with physical intimacy and much more to do with a kind of self-described "forever friendship." "They were the closest friendships I ever had, and they were technically with my exes," he said. At the time, nonmonogamy was an assumption in the gay community Thurow was part of. Now, he feels grateful that he lived his life with a family that broke all the boundaries around the traditional definition of the word.

"I must say, none of my straight friends get what this gay family thing is all about," Thurow said. He has experienced relationships as they change, and he sees value in all their iterations. "I tell my nephews when they break up with someone, 'You spent eight years with that woman; there was obviously something there. And now you're going to lose all that because you're not dating anymore?'" (Thurow, for the record, said that he doesn't really feel jealousy, so there's some indication that the Big Bad J-Word isn't so bad for all of us.)

When Thurow was describing his family structure to me, I couldn't stop thinking about Hannah—about how I could imagine spending a life with her in the kind of "forever friendship" he was describing. I thought back to those days when the last thing I wanted in the world was to see anyone or talk to anyone or do anything except watch trashy shows on TV and order a pizza and eat the entire thing, and then not throw the box away and fall asleep on the box so my dreams would smell like pizza. On those days, Hannah seemed to sense that I was in despair and didn't want to see her; she would gently coax me into the kitchen, saying that I didn't have to stay and talk too long. She would make salad. At first I wouldn't want to talk, and then, all of a sudden, I would. Hannah would listen and talk, and all that hurt would magically heal. This was pure magic. I wanted it in my life forever. I wished there was a way I could explain my feelings to her without making her feel pressured. I wondered if someday we might live in a community together like the ones I'd been reading about. The only thing that really sucks about Chicago is that Hannah isn't here.

But she did come to visit recently. She flew into O'Hare International Airport on a weekday; I left class early to take the hour-long train ride to meet her there. It wasn't the first time someone had visited me in Chicago; Luke and I had been in the Windy City for a year already. It was, however, the first time I'd gone out of my way to meet someone at the airport. I not only met Hannah at the airport but I also got there twenty minutes early and stood by the escalators waiting for her to come down. When I saw her, my heart skipped a beat like it did when my crush walked into my birthday party in second grade. Hannah was here! *Hannah!*

The feelings I had for Hannah were confusing to me. When we talked on the phone and one of us had to go, I felt like I'd been punched in the chest. Afterward, with the wind knocked out of me, I would think to myself, "Jesus, Sophie, get a grip! What's the big deal? Just call her again tomorrow!" This was strange because it was intense, even for me (and, if you haven't caught on by now, I have fairly intense emotions), and I haven't felt this way about any of the boys I've dated. Why did I miss Hannah so much? How could I explain this kind of love?

By the time Hannah got to Chicago, I'd made a list of things we could potentially do together, although I knew we wouldn't have time for even half of them. She would be staying for only two full days, and we both had work to finish that would prohibit us from spending every waking minute together. The place she wanted to go most, and the place I wanted to take her most, though, was the Garfield Park Conservatory— an enormous, free conservatory stacked to the gills with every kind of plant imaginable, and an outdoor area with an edible garden, a labyrinth, and a wall of carnivorous plants, among other growing green things.

Luke and I had been to the conservatory together twice—once to scope it out (it was better than we could have hoped), and the second time to see a corpse flower bloom. The week before Hannah was in town, Luke took Melissa to the conservatory while I was at work. If the conservatory had been in New Orleans, I think we would have gone at least thirty times over the course of a year, but Chicago is so much bigger and more spread out; there are too many things to do on a given day here. Mostly when we have free time, we go bird-watching outside. (We've become sort of amateur birders since we started dating.)

I couldn't really believe we'd lived in Chicago for a whole year. The day our lease began again, I printed out the email marking its renewal and read it to myself in bed a few times. To me, the lease was a symbol. I had been in an adult relationship—I had lived with a partner, and we had adopted cats and purchased joint furniture and built shelves—for an entire year. I lay in bed staring at this printed-out document and mused about whether or not I'd really changed all that much since I daydreamed about doing this with my first boyfriend. I felt like mostly the same person, but with some extra layers—like I was the centermost Russian nesting doll, now with a few added selves donned for protection.

But my relationship with Luke is vastly different from any of my other relationships. Relationships are collaborative chemistry; they're always weirdly at odds with the sum of their parts. Luke, who is ever the pragmatist even in moments of extreme crisis, mellows out my dramatic tendencies. I, on the other hand, encourage him to be emotional and to talk about his feelings. He doesn't want to grow up to be a writer or a stand-up comedian or a comic-book artist, and I don't want to grow up to be a manager at a YMCA or a diner owner, so there's nothing big for us to get competitive over. And Luke is so patient. It seems that this quality—inherent for him—is making me more patient, too.

The most significant difference between this relationship and every other relationship I've ever been in, of course, is that it's functionally polyamorous. Over the course of our first year in Chicago, a lot happened inside our polyamorous partnership—Luke says we've "leveled up" in the polysphere. Luke started seeing Melissa, and I continued to date Bob until he decided he wanted to be physically monogamous with the girl he fell in love with in New Orleans. I went on a few Tinder dates with a small assortment of people and then decided that I was too busy to be on Tinder for the time being. Also, Tinder wasn't resulting in the types of relationships I wanted to have; I was less interested in swiping right on a physical impulse and wanted instead to meet people who had already done a lot of thinking about polyamory before we went on dates.

The Ethical Slut and other polyamory primers often suggest setting up specific rules and guidelines to help map the anarchic world of open relationships. Luke and I forewent the map at first. I'd read a formative essay called "Loving Hard and Often" in the literary journal I edited. The anonymous writer advocated for romantic relationships without rules:

> Whether or not we sign contracts there are rules in place for how we interact with our parents, children, partners, teachers, clients and even our pets. We don't choose these rules. They are predetermined by powers that be in the interest of creating orderly, obedient

citizens and consumers. Friendship operates at the edges of these regulated relationships. Playing out both in public and in private, friendships allow us to regularly embrace fluidity and change. What's more romantic than that?[3]

After reading the essay, I vowed to let my love life exist without rules. This, however, had not been without its consequences. My brain made up its own rules (for example, "You won't fall in love with someone else; not really" and "You can't decide to stop sleeping with me"), and when the rules were violated, I was hurt without reasonable outward justification. After our five-hundredth discussion about jealousy, I realized that I probably needed some parameters for myself, but I couldn't figure out what they would be.

Luckily, a few months into our life together in Chicago, I met a polyamorous woman who introduced me to the concept of "parallel polyamory." The woman, Meg (remember Meg from the very beginning of this book?), was roughly my age but had been practicing polyamory since she was in college, and she was plugged into a whole network of polyamorous people who gathered regularly to schmooze and discuss theories about relationships and their many forms. Meg told me about dating someone who practiced parallel polyamory and that she hadn't done that before and wasn't necessarily into it. I had no idea what the term meant.

Of course, Meg was describing the only version of polyamory I really knew or understood. It was more closely connected to hookup culture than I realized, because it was primarily about having the explicit permission to engage in multiple relationships at once; in parallel polyamory, there is less emphasis on total transparency and honesty in love.

Parallel polyamory keeps a lot hidden. That was part of what had ultimately hurt my relationship with Jaedon; because Jaedon didn't really see me interact much with Luke, and those relationships were so separate (even though Luke and Jaedon were coworkers), it was hard for him to believe I was telling him the whole truth. And to be fair, I wasn't telling him the whole truth. I didn't want to hurt him, and I didn't want him to hurt me. And so, even though he knew I was dating Luke, he didn't quite trust the integrity of our relationship.

After I talked to Meg, I spent some time thinking about the kind of polyamory I wanted to practice, and I decided I didn't want to be in parallel polyamorous relationships anymore. I wanted to spend time with Melissa, and I wanted Luke to spend time with whomever I would date next. I wanted everything out in the open.

And I told him what Meg told me.

Luke was down to give this kind of relationship a try. Over a late Saturday brunch a few weeks later, he even upped the ante a little and said he was interested in dating another couple. Couples dating couples was a concept I'd read about in books about polyamory, and that the poly blogger Alan M. had talked to me about on the phone a little. (He and his wife are currently in a relationship with another couple. I didn't ask him too much about it, because at the time the idea was so foreign to me that I didn't even know where to begin.) In this relationship model, two people in a primary relationship go on a date with two other people in a primary relationship—and maybe they all get physical together. It's not unlike the idea of swinging that took off in the early 1970s, when newly married couples of the Free Love movement wanted to break the rules in a new way. I told Luke that that sounded fun to me, too, but it also sounded like a lot of work. I told him we could stay open to it, but I didn't know when we'd have the time to find another couple interested in going or even willing to go on a date with us.

And that was when the Magic of the Universe (or whatever you want to call it) stepped in, twisting the plot of our lives in a way that no self-respecting fiction novelist would ever write for fear of seeming too implausibly in sync. Just a few days after our brunch discussion, Luke and I were invited to a play party (read: a kink-friendly sex party) at Meg's apartment. We'd never been to a party like that before, but it was just the kind of thing we'd been hoping to try, and so we went. Although, don't get me wrong, we were nervous.

The play party was, importantly, a highly consent-driven and pri-marily sober affair. I mention sobriety here because, in my experience, wanting to experiment around sex is too often conflated with drinking alcohol and doing drugs. Luke and I are both currently nondrinkers, and we don't do drugs. We've talked a lot about it, because for both of us, sobriety is personally necessary to really engage in sexual exper-imentation. I want to be completely cognizant of my choices, and I want to make sure that I can both honestly give consent and under-stand when it is being given to me. I'm a little afraid of sounding too much like *A Preteen's Guide to Safe and Responsible Sex Parties*, but the correlation between rape and alcohol—roughly half of all incidents of sexual assault involve alcohol consumption—is too strong to be ignored or left out of a conversation like this.[4] I'm a survivor of sexual assault, and to be honest, the idea of a party like this had always terri-fied me. What if something someone did triggered me somehow? What if I failed to say no to something I didn't want to do and ended up regretting it? What if I said no *too* forcefully and made everyone in the room feel like I was overly sensitive? But Meg set up firm rules: every single physical transaction required explicit verbal consent; everyone who attended had to be personally vetted; and no late arrivals were permitted. We played a sexy game of truth or dare ("Kiss everyone in the room"; "What is one fantasy you'd like to live out tonight?"), and then everyone dispersed in pairs or more to, uh, play.

I started the night making out with Meg's live-in partner. He asked if he could kiss me; he asked if he could touch my waist; he asked if he could take off my glasses. After a while, I saw Luke across the room and asked him to join us. All my fear melted away right then. All night, everyone I interacted with asked about doing any and everything, and with each question I felt more self-assured. I also started to feel like my body was strong and beautiful and powerful. With all these people asking me if they could touch me or kiss me or hold me, I truly felt, for the first time in my entire life, that my body was desirable, and that it belonged only to me. There may have been times when I came close to feeling like that before, but they were nothing like this. I felt like a goddess.

After the party, Meg texted that she and her partner were interested in going on a date with Luke and me. It was as though she had been sitting at the table behind us that day at brunch and knew that we were interested in the idea of dating a couple. I asked Luke what he thought. Luke said he thought that a date with Meg and her partner sounded great; we were both attracted to both of them. And so it happened that Luke and I, as a couple, went on a romantic date with another couple—he and I, in some ways a single entity, united in our nervousness and excitement.

Our first date with Meg and Tony took place at their apartment. They made us broccoli and rice, and we sat on their big couches and talked and laughed for a few hours; then we went into their bedroom and made out with each other for a while. Everyone made out with everyone else. Everyone touched everyone else. Everyone kissed everyone else good-bye, and then Luke and I went home. We both thought it was really fun.

♡ ⌒ ♡ ⌒ ♡

The party and the text message and the newfound sense of polyamorous coupledom all took place the day before Hannah arrived for her visit. I felt happy and new; I had a fresh understanding of what love and sex could mean. It was the first time in a long time that my personal practice of polyamory had not involved even a shred of jealousy.

I felt evangelized. And, I felt, it was a great time to talk to Hannah about my feelings for her.

On the train to the Garfield Park Conservatory, I told Hannah all about the sexy party, and about Meg, and about how I felt like I'd broken through something significant in my personal exploration of love and self. Hannah's eyes widened as I told the story; she nodded and made little affirmative sounds. I remembered what a pleasure it was to tell Hannah a story like this in person. She was always so on board with whatever revelations I might have; she seemed so genuinely happy for me. It was the same way when I was sad about something—my job or a relationship or the state of the world; she seemed to carry some of my sadness. She had this gift for making me feel like she always shared my load.

So it felt like the most natural thing in the world to finish the story about the party and to lay my palm on Hannah's arm and say:

By the time I finished talking, we'd made it to the conservatory. Hannah suggested we go around the back to the labyrinth and sit by the bamboo behind it. It was the exact place Luke had suggested we sit the first time we visited. It was cold that day with Luke; we'd been wearing layers of coats and knit hats and gloves, but we liked the quiet of the outside, and we sat in silence and looked for winter birds. This time, with Hannah, the weather was warm. There was still kale sprouting up in the edible garden, and kids were running across the labyrinth, scream-laughing and tagging one another's shoulders. We lay in the grass, half-shaded by a gingko tree. Hannah held my hand.

And that was really all there was to say.

I don't know what love is. My love for Hannah and my love for Luke can both feel like they take up my whole body sometimes, more than hunger or thirst or pain or loneliness ever can. The way I love my sister, Alexis, and the way I love my mother are so similar and so different—and so similar and so different, too, from the way I still love Bob in New Orleans, or Kim from my first time in Chicago. When Jesse, who I still talk to on the phone, says "I love you" to me, the words carry something that seems bigger than life itself, but I couldn't possibly put my thumb on it. At Ben's wedding in October, I gave a speech and told dozens of people how the best person I knew had found the best person *he* knew, and the fact that they were so happy made me believe in something I thought I had grown too skeptical to believe in: the undeniable power of a single love.

But I'm not a person who's of a single love. I have many. And this, I think, is my great gift. It's my small—but mighty—reason for being. Everyone needs one, after all.

PART 8

Bird-Watching

There's a subtle distinction between birding and bird-watching (even if the dictionary doesn't recognize it). In a piece for *The New Yorker*, bird enthusiast Jonathan Rosen simplifies it thusly: "Crudely put, bird-watchers look at birds; birders look for them."[1] If this is true, then my mother and I are bird-watchers, and not birders. Luke is, too.

Luke got serious about bird-watching right after we started dating.The bird feeder I'd kept for years had broken, and I didn't feel like financially committing to a new one right then. I was about to donate a Costco-sized bag of birdseed to Goodwill when Luke saw it in the trunk of my car. He asked what it was. "It's birdseed, for bird watching," I said. He asked if he could have it, and I tried to gently break it to him that you couldn't bird watch without a ton of *gear*. He would need to invest in a big bird feeder, and he didn't even really have a good yard for it. He would probably want to get a suet feeder, too, because otherwise he'd be stuck with nothing but sparrows. But Luke wouldn't listen. He wanted the birdseed. One morning, after he'd made coffee, he opened the front doors of his house and threw a handful of birdseed onto the sidewalk. "That's not how you do it!" I protested. But in ten minutes, the birds came. Soon we spent every Sunday sitting on his front steps, throwing handfuls of birdseed at the common sparrows and wondering about how and why and where they would move.

The April after we met, Luke took me to the Grand Isle Migratory Bird Celebration. Grand Isle is pretty much the southernmost point of Louisiana—it's the end of the road for Louisiana Highway 1 and is the state's only inhabited island. Birds at the end of their tedious trek across the Gulf of Mexico love to hang out on Grand Isle for a few days in April; they rest and rejuvenate before dispersing farther north.

Luke and I decided to camp on the beach the night before we set out to see the birds. This was a bad idea, as there was a massive thunderstorm overnight and everything we brought with us was soaked. I could complain about that, but the fact that we weren't killed by a bolt of lightning (even though the metal poles on our tent were the tallest things around) was, by definition, a saving grace. The thunderstorm and subsequent flood kept us from really sleeping, but we had to get to the Bird Celebration headquarters at 6:00 a.m. to see the really good birds. When we arrived, we were not amused.

The thunderstorm hadn't passed overnight; it sagged across the island all day. We trudged through knee-deep water that splashed from every direction and got inside our raincoats. I put on a bathing suit. We continued to be extremely not amused.

But then we saw something that I will not be able to describe to you accurately, because it was more beautiful and magical than words have the capacity to tell. We saw a flock of maybe a hundred indigo buntings. An indigo bunting is a bird so all-over blue that you think it must have fallen into a bucket of paint when you see it. They rose up out of a bristly shrub in airy unison, as though they were all just one bird emitting a great sigh.

Birds flocking is really something special to watch. Magnificent waves of starlings tornadoing around city buildings or blankets of sparrows rising up out of the grass—there's just something about it that stuns you and makes you believe—even if just for a moment—in a Bigger Thing.

When I try to think about that ridiculous cloud of blue buntings flying together across the gigantic Gulf of Mexico, I can't wrap my brain around it. How do they know when to leave? Who decides? How do they map the route without Siri? How do they know where to stop? How can all those individual birds stay together for all that time? Of course they *have* to stay together in order to survive as a species; but *how do they do it?* If there was only one indigo bunting left in the entire world, would she know how to make the journey all by herself?

It's ultimately just as difficult to wrap my mind around the concept of polyamory. Morning Glory Zell-Ravenheart's definition of polyamory is the one that ended up in the Oxford English Dictionary: "The practice, state, or ability of having more than one sexual, loving relationship at the same time, with the full knowledge and consent of all partners involved." One Urban Dictionary user, however, outwardly rejects that definition, explaining that "In reality, polyamory is more often used as nothing more than a way of attempting to make 'open' relationships appear more mature by selfish individuals who use the idea of polyamory as a means to have multiple sexual partners while keeping the relationships themselves in an overly complicated and childish attrition."[2] People today define the word "polyamory" differently. It hasn't always been that way.

The universe of dating, love, family, and sex is evolving so quickly that our shared vernacular hasn't been able to keep up. As people form relationships that increasingly fall (in utterly disparate ways) into the "It's Complicated" box, we've struggled for a simple way to describe them. If Rory is seriously dating Sir Rory, but Sir Rory is allowed to sleep with three other girls, what is that? And if Rory is sleeping with Rory 2 but not having sex with her, and Sir Rory is having sex with both Rory and Rory 2 but neither of them knows about the other's affair with Sir Rory, what is *that*? As everyone flounders in redefining the word "relationship," "polyamory" has been forced to be the one-size-fits-all garment. And as with any single article of clothing, if something is worn too much and by too many, it gets stretched out.

Zell-Ravenheart's "polyamory" and the Urban Dictionary user's definition are actually perfect opposites—just as "birding" and "bird-watching" can be. The key difference in each case, perhaps, has to do with control.

Rosen writes, "Bird watching is really all about the quest for balance—between the curious animal at the near end of the binoculars and the wild animal at the far end; between the classifiable and the ineffably mysterious; between our killing, conquering urges and our impulse toward conservation."[3] It's an unsteady road, because there's no obvious indicator as to whether you're veering too far one way or the other. Anapol writes, likewise, that "polyamory is not an identity that dictates having multiple partners but rather a fluid process of checking in with oneself to see what feels appropriate with a given person in a given situation."[4] This is a similarly unsure path. It asks that human beings behave like rivers—that is, moving forward and trusting the flow—and not like human beings. Humans like to control things. That's why John James Audubon, perhaps the most celebrated birder of all time, killed hundreds of thousands of the birds he said he loved in order to categorize them, classify them, and paint them into place.

Polyamory (the first definition) provides no answers; only more questions. You have to decide if that's the kind of love life you want to have. Curiosity can actually be quite terrifying—especially when there aren't any true answers. But then sometimes curiosity leads you to being knee-deep in rainwater watching a completely ridiculous, brilliant blue swirl of birds rise up before you.

♡ ～ ♡ ⌣ ♡

I didn't see an indigo bunting again until almost three years later. Luke and I were in our Chicago apartment in the middle of May. My birthday had just passed; I'd completed graduate school, and my parents had come and gone to celebrate it all. Our apartment was finally quiet, and Luke had asked me a few weeks prior if I could reserve this particular Saturday for him; he said things had been so busy, and he just wanted to spend the day with me. In the morning, we drank coffee and gazed out the window at our bird feeder. In Chicago, early May is peak birding season (and, for us, peak bird-watching season). Migratory birds, on their way farther north, have a kind of spring break in Chicago before taking on Lake Michigan. Just as humans do on spring break, the birds have lots and lots of sex. Since they're in sexy moods, the male birds (warblers, mostly) wear their migratory plumage—butter-yellows and apple-reds that seem to have come out of a child's box of crayons. Mostly, the rarer birds don't come to our feeder. We had the usual cast of house sparrows and mourning doves, with a goldfinch here and there. So it was pure magic that on this mid-May Saturday, an indigo bunting showed up at the feeder like it was no big thing at all.

An INDIGO BUNTING at the feeder

like it AIN'T NO THING.

We sat and watched it for half an hour. It seemed like a sort of accident: how could one tiny bird be so blue? Luke said we should go out to the lakefront and see what other birds were out, so we rode our bikes to the lake. It had been raining for seven straight days, but this Saturday was sunny and warm, and the birds were apparently happy for a dry morning (with lots of post-rain bugs to eat). The birders were out en masse at the bird sanctuary near our house. They'd set up their ridiculous scopes and were whisper-yelling things to each other like "Oh my god, it's a G-D mourning warbler" and "It's either a yellow-rumped or a magnolia, but I can't tell." We didn't need to name the birds, but we spent a few hours appreciating them from our distance. One woman said to us,

We lingered longer than usual, because something about this day felt sort of enchanted. You know those dating montages in movies in

which the in-love characters keep laughing and running around even when one of the characters spills their ice cream or it starts raining? It was a day like that. We sat on the lip of the lake and listened to an amateur saxophone player wail badly (but charmingly) into the wind. We watched him explain to a school-aged girl how the air moved into and out of the instrument; I let my ear rest on Luke's shoulder. Just as I'd felt during my first kiss ever, I actively wished I could stop time. I felt so pleased that a clichéd, childish wish like that could still exist in my thirties.

I daydreamed about eating tacos and napping the afternoon away as we biked home. But that was before I got to the front door of our apartment. Because when I got to the front door of our apartment, I understood that I wouldn't remember this day for the saxophone player or the snobby birders, or even for the indigo bunting. Our plastic Mardi Gras cups were lined up on the doorstep, and someone had planted yellow daisies inside them. I don't know about you, but yellow daisies make me think of just one thing: season one, episode twenty-one of *Gilmore Girls*.

In the episode, Lorelai tells her boyfriend, Max, that for a marriage proposal, "There should be a thousand yellow daisies." Then one day she comes to work to find that someone's delivered a thousand yellow daisies—they fill the room, and it's totally startling. I love yellow, I love daisies, and I love *Gilmore Girls*. Even though Lorelai and Max don't ultimately end up together, I've always agreed that for a marriage proposal, there should be a thousand yellow daisies.

I unlocked the front door of the apartment and walked into the front hall. Yellow daisies lining the hallway. Yellow daisies on all the bookshelves. Yellow daisies on the hope chest and on the windowsill. And in the living room, huge pots of yellow daisies, joined with other flowers of every type: marigolds, foxgloves, pansies, forget-me-nots, the works. There weren't just a thousand; there were thousands. When I turned around to look at Luke, he was on one knee, holding a little black box just like in all the rom-coms I'm supposed to hate.

The ring was an Oregon sunstone.

"Because you hate diamonds, you love Oregon, & you're afraid of the dark," he said.

I always imagined how gracefully I'd say yes if anyone ever proposed to me. A single tear would trickle down my powdered cheek, and I'd nod vehemently before Prince Charming rose to his feet to lift me and twirl me around. In real life, I fell on top of Luke and sobbed with all the poise of a bridge troll. I snotted on his shirt. I wailed something about loving him so much and chewed on his nose in a dizzy stab at a kiss.

We had sex as engaged people. People called us to say congratulations—his dad called *while* we were naked in bed, and Luke (ever the neophyte with technology) didn't realize it was a Facetime call. We had brunch at our favorite neighborhood joint (I just call it "the mushroom restaurant" because they have many mushroom dishes). After the mushroom restaurant, we had sex again as engaged people.

That night, Luke had one more surprise planned. He'd gotten tickets to see a Sarah Ruhl play called *For Peter Pan on Her 70th Birthday*, and he'd invited Meg and Tony to join us.

Sarah Ruhl authored the first Off-Broadway play about polyamory. *How to Transcend a Happy Marriage* premiered at Lincoln Center in 2017; Luke and I flew to New York to see it.

We sat in the front row, and afterward walked down the street to an all-night diner to talk. I was eager to tell this couple I loved about my engagement. It went without saying that the engagement wouldn't change anything between us—except that now Luke and I wanted Meg and Tony to come to a party celebrating our love. I knew Meg and Tony wouldn't need to ask the question that some of my family members would have: "So, if you're polyamorous, why are you getting married?" The answer, to them, was as obvious as it was to us. We wanted to get married because we were committed to each other for life. It's as simple as that.

After the day was over, I lay in bed wondering how it was that I'd gotten so lucky. I mean, this man *deeply* understood the importance of sunstones and cheap tacos and bird-watching and so, so many other things. On a whim, just then, I decided to ask him why he liked bird-watching. His answer was as simple as they come.

Acknowledgments

Mackenzie Brady Watson is a literal superhuman who soared into my life and made it infinitely better in millions of ways. Obviously, this book would not exist without her. I would not be who I am without her. I love her.

Jill Riddell was my graduate school advisor, who told me to "be brave" and "try a longer work," which I had had no intention of ever doing. She read this book more times than I did, and when I was finished with it, she gave me zucchini bread. I love her.

Cara Bedick and Lara Blackman were the two most patient editors I could possibly imagine working with. I'm not an easy person. Lara and Cara made calm cooing noises at me while simultaneously whipping this manuscript into shape. I love them.

Alexis Gargagliano edited the earliest iterations of this text, and she shaped a lot of stray fragments into something at least marginally readable. I love her.

Then there are the hordes of others upon whom I have forced pages. These people generously read the pages and gave gentle criticism, knowing that I'm extremely thin-skinned. I love every one of these people. Here are some of their names: Sam Alden, Ann Calcagno, Rachel Cromidas, Leah Fishbein, Mary Fons, Loretta Johnson, Alex Kerr, Rachel Lee, Jesse LeMon, Louisa Leontiades, Alan M., Peggy Macnamara, Ned Moore, Kim Neer, Eli Piatt, Derek Roguski, Hannah Sadtler, Mac Schubert, Hannah Sherrard, Jessica Thompson, Chuck Thurow, Bob Weisz, and Valerie White. There are definitely names I'm forgetting. I love all those people, too.

My mom is more incredible than I've let on in these pages. Throughout this process, she's been vulnerable, honest, and accepting. If I grow up to be just like her, I will have exceeded my wildest expectations for myself. I love her. My dad, despite his relative absence from this text, is pretty awesome, too. I also love him.

My sister, Alexis, is my greatest life love. It's strange, in some ways, that in a book called *Many Love* she would not come up more. The love I share with my sister is sacred and deserves its own book. Nevertheless, Alexis has put up with a lot of whining and complaining while I've written this one. I love her.

And finally: I never imagined I would meet a human like Luke Hoar de Galvan. He is just as thoughtful, kind, gracious, intelligent, and generally wonderful as I've tried to portray. He took me out for vegan doughnuts every time something went wrong with this book—and I'll just say that there were a *lot* of vegan doughnuts. Luke listened dutifully to all my grievances and stayed up late into the night with me while I inked illustrations until my hands hurt. He cleaned up after me, he cooked for me, and he championed me. He is an actual earth angel. I love him more than I have words for.

Notes

FAQ

1 Alan M., "Deborah Taj Anapol, 1951–2015," *Polyamory in the News!*, August 19, 2015, http://polyinthemedia.blogspot.com/2015/08/deborah-taj -anapol-1951-2015.html.

2 Deborah Anapol, *Polyamory in the 21st Century: Love and Intimacy with Multiple Partners* (Lanham, MD: Rowman & Littlefield, 2010), 206.

Chapter 1: Happily Ever After?

1 Cindy Hazan and Phillip R. Shaver, "Attachment as an Organizational Framework for Research on Close Relationships," *Psychological Inquiry* 5, no. 1 (1994): 1–22.

2 Wyndol Furman, "The Emerging Field of Adolescent Romantic Relationships," *Current Directions in Psychological Science* 11, no. 5 (October 2002): 177–80.

3 Rachel Martin, "Sorting Through the Numbers on Infidelity," NPR, July 26, 2015, https://www.npr.org/2015/07/26/426434619/sorting-through-the-numbers -on-infidelity.

4 "Why People Cheat: 'The Normal Bar' Reveals Infidelity Causes," *Huffington Post*, January 22, 2013, https://www.huffingtonpost.com/2013/01/22/why -people-cheat_n_2483371.html.

5 Martin, "Sorting Through the Numbers on Infidelity."

6 University of Guelph, "Sexual Anxiety, Personality Predictors of Infidelity, Study Says," *ScienceDaily*, July 26, 2011, https://www.sciencedaily.com /releases/2011/07/110725123411.htm.

7 Peggy Orenstein, *Girls & Sex: Navigating the Complicated New Landscape* (New York: HarperCollins, 2016), 73.

8 "Box Office History for Romantic Comedy," The Numbers, https://www .the-numbers.com/market/genre/Romantic-Comedy.

9 Natalie Angier, "The Changing American Family," *New York Times*, Novem-

ber 25, 2013, http://www.nytimes.com/2013/11/26/health/families.html ?pagewanted=all&_r=0.

10 Amy Davidson Sorkin, "A Guide to Guerrilla Parenting," *The New Yorker*, August 1, 2016, https://www.newyorker.com/magazine/2016/08/01/parenting-in-an-age-of-economic-anxiety.

Chapter 2: "Just" "Friends"

1 Julie Beck, "How Friendships Change in Adulthood," *The Atlantic*, October 22, 2015.

2 Randy Newman, "You've Got a Friend in Me," *Toy Story*, Walt Disney Records, 1995, https://www.youtube.com/watch?v=Zy4uiiy0qgA.

3 Plato, *Symposium*, trans. Benjamin Jowett, http://classics.mit.edu/Plato /symposium.html.

4 "Fair Youth Sonnets," Hudson Shakespeare Company, http://hudsonshake-speare.org/Shakespeare%20Library/Poetry/Young%20Man%20sonnets.htm.

5 Jen Kim, "Sorry, But This Is Why You Can't Be Friends with Your Ex," *Psychology Today*, https://www.psychologytoday.com/blog/valley-girl-brain/201211 /sorry-is-why-you-can-t-be-friends-your-ex.

6 Amy L. Busboom, Dawn M. Collins, Michelle D. Givertz, and Lauren A. Levin, "Can We Still Be Friends? Resources and Barriers to Friendship Quality after Romantic Relationship Dissolution," *Personal Relationships* 9, no. 2 (June 2002): 215–23.

7 Sandra Metts, William R. Cupach, and Richard A. Bejlovec, "'I Love You Too Much to Ever Start Liking You': Redefining Romantic Relationships," *Journal of Social and Personal Relationships* 6, no. 3 (August 1, 1989): 259–74.

8 Susan Song, "Polyamory and Queer Anarchism: Infinite Possibilities for Resistance," in C. B. Daring, J. Rogue, Deric Shannon, and Abbey Volcano, eds., *Queering Anarchism: Essays on Gender, Power, and Desire* (Oakland, CA: AK Press, 2012), http://theanarchistlibrary.org/library/susan-song-polyamory -and-queer-anarchism-infinite-possibilities-for-resistance.

9 Anapol, *Polyamory in the 21st Century*, 61.

10 Andie Nordgren, *The Short Instructional Manifesto for Relationship Anarchy*, Anarchist Library, 2006, https://theanarchistlibrary.org/library/andie-nordgren -the-short-instructional-manifesto-for-relationship-anarchy.

11 Dean Spade, "For Lovers and Fighters," in Melody Berger, ed., *We Don't Need Another Wave: Dispatches from the Next Generation of Feminists* (New York: Seal Press, 2006), http://www.makezine.enoughenough.org/newpoly2 .html.

12 Anapol, *Polyamory in the 21st Century*, 5.

13 Ibid., 10.

14 Jean Baker Miller, PhD, and Irene Pierce Stiver, PhD, *The Healing Connec-*

tion: How Women Form Relationships in Therapy and in Life (Boston: Beacon Press, 2015), 35.

15   Ibid., 36.

16   Deborah Anapol, "Polyamory without Tears," *Psychology Today*, November 1, 2011, https://www.psychologytoday.com/blog/love-without-limits/201111 /polyamory-without-tears.

Chapter 3: Casual Love

1   Kelly Cooper, "A Woman's Advantage," OkCupid, March 5, 2015, www .okcupid.com/deep-end/a-womans-advantage.

Chapter 4: Let's Talk about Sex

1   Dossie Easton and Janet W. Hardy, *The Ethical Slut: A Practical Guide to Poly-amory, Open Relationships & Other Adventures*, 2nd ed. (Berkeley, CA: Celestial Arts, 2009), 4.

2   Peggy Orenstein, *Girls & Sex: Navigating the Complicated New Landscape* (New York: HarperCollins, 2016), 2.

3   Zoe Ruderman, "15 Women Describe What an Orgasm Feels Like to Them," *Cosmopolitan*, June 19, 2017, http://www.cosmopolitan.com/sex-love/advice /g1551/what-an-orgasm-feels-like/.

4   Dan Savage, "Savage Love: Basics, Bitches," *The Stranger*, November 20, 2013, https://www.thestranger.com/seattle/SavageLove?oid=18262632.

5   Sexuality Information and Education Council of the United States (SIECUS), "A History of Federal Funding for Abstinence-Only-Until-Marriage Pro-grams," http://www.siecus.org/index.cfm?fuseaction=page.viewpage&pageid =1340&nodeid=1.

6   Nancy Jo Sales, "Tinder and the Dawn of the 'Dating Apocalypse,'" *Vanity Fair*, August 6, 2015, https://www.vanityfair.com/culture/2015/08/tinder -hook-up-culture-end-of-dating.

7   Karley Sciortino, "Breathless: In Defense of Hookup Culture," *Vogue*, September 9, 2015, https://www.vogue.com/article/breathless-karley-sciortino -hookup-culture-casual-sex.

Chapter 5: Many Love

1   Sophie Lucido Johnson, "TOUR Day 7—Los Angeles and Polyamory," *Sophie Lucido Johnson* (blog), August 8, 2014, http://www.sophielucidojohnson.com /blogblog/2014/8/8/tour-day-7-los-angeles-and-polyamory?rq=polyamory.

Chapter 6: Jealousy

1 David M. Buss, PhD, *The Dangerous Passion: Why Jealousy Is as Necessary as Love and Sex* (New York: Free Press, 2000), 206.
2 Christopher Ryan and Cacilda Jethá, *Sex at Dawn: The Prehistoric Origins of Modern Sexuality* (New York: HarperCollins, 2010), 139.
3 Ibid., 143–44.
4 Ibid., 148.
5 Anapol, *Polyamory in the 21st Century*, 112.
6 Ronald Mazur, *The New Intimacy: Open-Ended Marriage and Alternative Life-styles* (Bloomington, IN: iUniverse, 2000), 98.
7 Ibid., 100–112.
8 Amanda Holman and Alan Sillars, "Talk about 'Hooking Up': The Influence of College Student Social Networks on Nonrelationship Sex," *Health Communication* 27, no. 2 (2012): 205–16.

Chapter 7: Relationships without Borders

1 Louisa Leontiades, "Poly Parenting: 30 Days to Clarity & Confidence When You're Raising Small Children," LouisaLeontiades.com, http://louisaleontiades.com/30-days-to-clarity-on-your-parenting-problem/.
2 Robert Fieseler, Cassie Harvey, and Marina Lopes, "Open House: Inside a New Kind of Family," Atavist.com, June 18, 2013, https://openhouse.atavist.com/.
3 Anonymous, "Loving Hard and Often," *Neutrons/Protons*, May 31, 2015, http://neutronsprotons.com/2015/05/31/loving-hard-and-often-2/.
4 Antonia Abbey, PhD; Tina Zawacki, MA; Philip O. Buck, MA; A. Monique Clinton, MA; and Pam McAuslan, PhD, "Alcohol and Sexual Assault," National Institute on Alcohol Abuse and Alcoholism, National Institutes of Health, https://pubs.niaaa.nih.gov/publications/arh25-1/43-51.htm.

Chapter 8: Bird-Watching

1 Jonathan Rosen, "The Difference Between Bird Watching and Birding," *The New Yorker*, October 17, 2011, https://www.newyorker.com/books/page-turner/the-difference-between-bird-watching-and-birding.
2 "Polyamory," Urban Dictionary, https://www.urbandictionary.com/define.php?term=Polyamory.
3 Rosen, "The Difference Between Bird Watching and Birding."
4 Anapol, *Polyamory in the 21st Century*, 87.

Bibliography

Abbey, Antonia, PhD, Tina Zawacki, MA, Philip O. Buck, MA, A. Monique Clinton, MA, and Pam McAuslan, PhD. "Alcohol and Sexual Assault." National Institutes of Health. https://pubs.niaaa.nih.gov/publications/arh25-1/43-51.htm.

Anapol, Deborah M. *Polyamory in the 21st Century: Love and Intimacy with Multiple Partners.* Lanham, MD: Rowman & Littlefield Publishers, 2010.

Ananthaswamy, Anil. "Hormones Converge for Couples in Love." *New Scientist,* May 5, 2004.

Anderson, Monica. "Teen Voices: Dating in the Digital Age." Pew Research Center. October 1, 2015. http://www.pewinternet.org/online-romance/.

Angier, Natalie. "The Changing American Family." *New York Times,* November 25, 2013. http://www.nytimes.com/2013/11/26/health/families.html.

Anonymous. "Loving Hard and Often." *Neutrons Protons,* May 31, 2015. http://neutronsprotons.com/2015/05/31/loving-hard-and-often-2/.

Aristotle, W. D. Ross, and J. O. Urmson. *The Nicomachean Ethics.* Oxford, UK: Oxford University Press, 1980.

Aughinbaugh, Alison, Omar Robies, and Hugette Sun. "Marriage and Divorce: Patterns by Gender, Race, and Educational Attainment." *Monthly Labor Review,* October 2013.

Bachman, J. G., L. D. Johnston, and P. M. O'Malley. *Monitoring the Future: A Continuing Study of American Youth* (8th-, 10th-, and 12th-Grade Surveys), 1976–2012. Conducted by University of Michigan Survey Research Center. ICPSR ed. Ann Arbor, MI: Inter-university Consortium for Political and Social Research [producer and distributor].

Beck, Julie. "How Friendships Change in Adulthood." *The Atlantic,* October 22, 2015.

Belam, Martin, and Eleni Stefanou. "What Is Love—Can It Really Be Defined and Explained?" *The Guardian* (UK), February 12, 2016. https://www.theguardian.com/lifeandstyle/2016/feb/12/what-is-love-valentines-day-experts.

Brookshire, Bethany. "Dopamine Is _____." *Slate,* July 3, 2013. http://www.slate.com/articles/health_and_science/science/2013/07/what_is_dopamine_love_lust_sex_addiction_gambling_motivation_reward.html.

Bugler, Caroline. *The Bird in Art.* London: Merrell, 2012.

Burns, April, Valerie A. Futch, and Deborah L. Tolman. "It's Like Doing Home-work." *Sexuality Research and Social Policy* 8, no. 3 (2011): 239–51.

Busboom, A. L., D. M. Collins, M. D. Givertz, and L. A. Levin. "Can We Still Be Friends? Resources and Barriers to Friendship Quality after Romantic Rela-tionship Dissolution." *Personal Relationships* 9 (2002): 215–23.

Buss, David M. *The Dangerous Passion: Why Jealousy Is as Necessary as Love and Sex.* New York: Free Press, 2000.

Centers for Disease Control and Prevention. "National Marriage and Divorce Rate Trends." National Center for Health Statistics, November 23, 2015. https://www.cdc.gov/nchs/nvss/marriage_divorce_tables.htm.

Clark, Russell. "Gender Differences in Receptivity to Sexual Offers." *Jour-nal of Psychology & Human Sexuality* 2, no. 1 (1989): 39–55. doi:10.1300 /j056v02n01_04.

Davidson, Amy. "Parental Controls." *The New Yorker*, August 1, 2016, 65–67.

DePaulo, Bella, PhD. "Ditched by Friend Who Got Married: Can You Relate?" *Psychology Today*, September 7, 2011. https://www.psychologytoday.com /blog/living-single/201109/ditched-friend-who-got-married-can-you -relate.

———. "The New Science of Friendship." *Psychology Today*, December 9, 2012. https://www.psychologytoday.com/blog/living-single/201212/the-new -science-friendship.

Easton, Dossie, and Janet W. Hardy. *The Ethical Slut: A Practical Guide to Poly-amory, Open Relationships & Other Adventures.* Berkeley, CA: Celestial Arts, 2009.

Fieseler, Robert, Cassie Harvey, and Marina Lopes. *Open House: Inside a New Kind of Family.* Self-Published. https://openhouse.atavist.com.

Figes, Kate. "The Infidelity Epidemic: Never Have Marriage Vows Been Under So Much Strain." *Daily Mail*, April 19, 2013. http://www.dailymail.co.uk/news /article-2311947/The-infidelity-epidemic-Never-marriage-vows-strain -Relationship-expert-Kate-Figes-spent-3-years-finding-adultery-worryingly -common.html.

Furman, Wyndol. "The Emerging Field of Adolescent Romantic Relationships." *Current Directions in Psychological Science* 11, no. 5 (2002): 177–80.

Furman, Wyndol, and Elizabeth A. Wehrner. "Adolescent Romantic Relation-ships: A Developmental Perspective." In Shmuel, Shulman, and W. Andrew Collins, eds. *Romantic Relationships in Adolescence.* San Francisco: Jossey-Bass Publishers, 1997, 21–36.

Garcia, Justin R., Chris Reiber, Sean G. Massey, and Ann M. Merriwether. "Sex-ual Hookup Culture: A Review." *Review of General Psychology* 16, no. 2 (2012): 161–76.

Grohol, John M., PsyD. "How Common Is Cheating & Infidelity Really?" *World of Psychology*, 2013. http://psychcentral.com/blog/archives/2013/03/22 /how-common-is-cheating-infidelity-really/.

Harrell, Eben. "Are Romantic Comedies Bad for You?" *Time*, December 23, 2008. http://content.time.com/time/health/article/0,8599,1868389,00.html.

Hazan, Cindy, and Phillip R. Shaver. "Attachment as an Organizational Framework for Research on Close Relationships." *Psychological Inquiry* 5, no. 1 (1994): 1–22.

Hefner, Veronica, and Barbara J. Wilson. "From Love at First Sight to Soul Mate: The Influence of Romantic Ideals in Popular Films on Young People's Beliefs about Relationships." *Communication Monographs* (2013).

Holman, Amanda, and Alan Sillars. "Talk About 'Hooking Up': The Influence of College Student Social Networks on Nonrelationship Sex." *Health Communication* 27, no. 2 (2012): 205–16.

Holmes, B. M. "In Search of My 'One and Only': Romance-oriented Media and Beliefs in Romantic Relationships Destiny." *Electronic Journal of Communication* 5, no. 3 (2007).

Kim, Jen. "Sorry, But This Is Why You Can't Be Friends with Your Ex." *Psychology Today*, November 29, 2012. https://www.psychologytoday.com/blog/valley -girl-brain/201211/sorry-is-why-you-can-t-be-friends-your-ex.

Kross, E., M. G. Berman, W. Mischel, E. E. Smith, and T. D. Wager. "Social Rejection Shares Somatosensory Representations with Physical Pain." *Proceedings of the National Academy of Sciences* 108, no. 15 (2011): 6270– 75.

Lawler, Joseph. "Women Are Having Fewer Kids, and Demographers Don't Know Why." *Washington Examiner*, June 7, 2014. http://www.washingtonexam- iner.com/women-are-having-fewer-kids-and-demographers-dont-know -why/article/2549445.

Leontiades, Louisa. "Poly Parenting: 30 Days to Clarity & Confidence When You're Raising Small Children." LouisaLeontiades.com. http://louisaleon- tiades.com/30-days-to-clarity-on-your-parenting-problem/.

Levine, Irene S., PhD. "For Better or For Worse: Weddings and Friendship." *Fractured Friendships*, February 9, 2009. http://www.fracturedfriendships.com /blog/better-or-worse-weddings-and-friendship.

M, Alan. "Building the Poly Movement." Address, Rocky Mountain Poly Living Convention, Denver, Colorado, April 15, 2016.

———. "Deborah Taj Anapol, 1951–2015." *Polyamory in the News!*, August 19, 2015. http://polyinthemedia.blogspot.com/2015/08/deborah-taj-anapol-1951-2015 .html.

Marazziti, D., H. S. Akiskal, A. Rossi, and G. B. Cassano. "Alteration of the Platelet Serotonin Transporter in Romantic Love." *Psychological Medicine* 29, no. 3 (1999): 741–45.

Mark, Kristen P., Erick Janssen, and Robin R. Milhausen. "Infidelity in Heterosexual Couples: Demographic, Interpersonal, and Personality-Related Predictors of Extradyadic Sex." *Archives of Sexual Behavior* 40, no. 5 (2011): 971–82.

Martin, Rachel. "Sorting through the Numbers on Infidelity." Transcript. *Weekend Edition Sunday*. NPR. July 26, 2015.

Mazur, Ronald Michael. *The New Intimacy: Open-Ended Marriage and Alternative Lifestyles*. Boston: Beacon Press, 1973.

Meeker, Margaret J. *Epidemic: How Teen Sex Is Killing Our Kids*. Washington, DC: LifeLine Press, 2002.

Meighan, Clement W. "Prehistoric Rock Paintings in Baja California." *American Antiquity* 31, no. 3 (1966): 372.

Metts, S., W. R. Cupach, and R. A. Bejlovec. "'I Love You Too Much to Ever Start Liking You': Redefining Romantic Relationships." *Journal of Social and Personal Relationships* 6, no. 3 (1989): 259–74.

Miller, Jean Baker., and Irene P. Stiver. *The Healing Connection: How Women Form Relationships in Therapy and in Life*. Boston: Beacon Press, 1997.

Morin, Rich. "The Public Renders a Split Verdict on Changes in Family Structure." Pew Research Center's Social & Demographic Trends Project. 2011. http://www.pewsocialtrends.org/2011/02/16/the-public-renders-a-split -verdict-on-changes-in-family-structure/?src=family-interactive.

Nash Information Services. "Box Office History for Romantic Comedy: Ticket Sales and Market Share by Year." 2016. http://www.the-numbers.com/market /genre/Romantic-Comedy.

Nordgren, Andie. "The Short Instructional Manifesto for Relationship Anarchy." *Andie's Log*, July 6, 2012. http://log.andie.se/post/26652940513/the-short -instructional-manifesto-for-relationship.

Northrup, Chrisanna, Pepper Schwartz, and James Witte. *The Normal Bar: The Surprising Secrets of Happy Couples and What They Reveal about Creating a New Normal in Your Relationship*. New York: Harmony Books, 2012.

Nutnot, Wayne. "I'm a Feminist, But I Don't Eat Pussy." Thought Catalog, July 7, 2013. http://thoughtcatalog.com/wayne-nutnot/2013/06/im-a-feminist -but-i-dont-eat-pussy/.

OkCupid. "A Woman's Advantage." *Deep End*, March 2016. https://www.okcupid .com/deep-end/a-womans-advantage.

Orenstein, Peggy. *Girls & Sex: Navigating the Complicated New Landscape*. New York: HarperCollins, 2016.

Plato, Benjamin Jowett, and Hayden Pelliccia. *Symposium: The Benjamin Jowett Translation*. New York: Modern Library, 1996.

Plotz, David. "This Is the Last Time I Will Ever See You." *Slate*, June 12, 2013. http://www.slate.com/articles/life/weddings/2013/06/wedding_guest_good- byes_friendships_that_end_after_your_wedding.html.

"Polyamory." *Oxford English Dictionary*, 2015. Accessed January 2, 2017. http:// oed.com.

Rosen, Jonathan. "The Difference Between Bird Watching and Birding." *The New Yorker*, October 16, 2014. http://www.newyorker.com/books/page-turner /the-difference-between-bird-watching-and-birding.

Ruderman, Zoe. "What the Big O Feels Like for Me." *Cosmopolitan*, 2016. Accessed January 2, 2017. http://www.cosmopolitan.com/sex-love/advice /g1551/what-an-orgasm-feels-like/.

Ryan, Christopher, and Cacilda Jethá. *Sex at Dawn: The Prehistoric Origins of Modern Sexuality*. New York: HarperCollins, 2010.

Sales, Nancy Jo, and Justin Bishop. "Tinder and the Dawn of the Dating Apocalypse." *Vanity Fair*, September 2016. http://www.vanityfair.com/culture /2015/08/tinder-hook-up-culture-end-of-dating.

Sandberg, Sheryl. *Lean In: Women, Work, and the Will to Lead*. London: WH Allen, 2014.

Sciortino, Karley. "Breathless: In Defense of Hookup Culture." *Vogue*, September 9, 2015. http://www.vogue.com/13332301/breathless-karley-sciortino -hookup-culture-casual-sex/.

Sexual Information and Education Council of the United States. "A History of Federal Funding for Abstinence-Only-Until-Marriage Programs." SIECUS, 2012. http://www.siecus.org/index.cfm?fuseaction=page.viewpage&%3B-pageid=1340&%3Bnodeid=1.

Shakespeare, William, A. C. Curtis, and Sandro Botticelli. *Sonnets*. Guildford, UK: A.C. Curtis, 1902.

Spade, Dean. "For Lovers and Fighters." Make Zine, 2006. http://www.makezine .enoughenough.org/newpoly2.html.

Tan, K., C. R. Agnew, L. E. Vanderdrift, and S. M. Harvey. "Committed to Us: Predicting Relationship Closeness Following Nonmarital Romantic Relationship Breakup." *Journal of Social and Personal Relationships* 32, no. 4 (2014): 456–71. doi:10.1177/0265407514536293.

Time, September 11, 2015.

United States Census Bureau. "Quick Facts: Chicago, Illinois." 2016 United States Census. http://www.census.gov/quickfacts/table/LND110210/1714000.

Way, Mish Barber. "Men Explain, in Great Detail, Why They Won't Eat Pussy." *Broadly*, March 30, 2016. https://broadly.vice.com/en_us/article/men-explain -in-great-detail-why-they-dont-eat-pussy.

INDEX

About the Author

Sophie Lucido Johnson is a writer, illustrator, and comedian. She has been published in *The New Yorker*, *Guernica*, the *Guardian*, *Vice*, *Catapult*, *Dame*, *McSweeney's*, *Jezebel*, *The Hairpin*, *The Nation*, and *Rookie*, among others, with much of her writing on the subject of open relationships. She holds an MFAW at the School of the Art Institute of Chicago. *Many Love* is her first book.